EMBALMED ALIVE!

Louis H. Valbracht, D.D.

EMBALMED ALIVE!

ISBN 0-89536-277-5

PRINTED IN U.S.A.

To The Rev. Frederick J. Weertz, D.D. and The Rev. Alfred J. Beil, D.D., who, as Pastor and Associate Pastor, over the decades preceding my ministry, laid the firm foundation, Jesus Christ being the chief cornerstone, on which we have continued to build at St. John's Lutheran Church in Des Moines, Iowa.

CONTENTS

The Unemployed Embalmers

Renan, the French Skeptic, scathingly quipped that the Christian faith was built on the body of a dead Jew. He was right, at least as far as the first resurrection morn.

It's a strange anachronism that we customarily have Sunrise Services on Easter morning, and shake our sanctuaries with the sound of victorious alleluias. Very conveniently we've twisted the facts. Those who appeared on the first Easter were, they were sure, dealing with nothing but the body of a dead Jew. They were hastening to finish the gruesome job of embalming it. They have left behind them a deadly heritage. Generation after generation, for close to 2,000 years, their strain persists. There are still a host of persons who can think of nothing to do with life except mummify it.

How do people in stories become glamorized in the telling and retelling? How do we make heroes out of heels, wise men out of fools, ladies out of tramps, successes out of failures? Even in Al Capp's "Li'l Abner," that cutting satire of all of our human failings and foibles, he depicts Dogpatch's own General Cornpone. General Cornpone, of course, was the leader of Cornpone's Defeat, Cornpone's Retreat, Cornpone's Route, Cornpone's Folly, Cornpone's Mistake, Cornpone's Debacle, and Cornpone's Disaster. And yet, the people of Dogpatch erected a monument in his memory and made of him a hero.

And it occurred to me that that is exactly what we do with the story of Easter, the first morning of the Resurrection. I have read, and heard, and even preached sermons that started out with that little embalming party leaving their homes in the cold light of dawn and hurrying to the Garden of Joseph of Arimathea to the tomb where the body of the crucified Christ had been hastily buried. Bent they were on their sad and somewhat gruesome mission of preparing that body for permanent burial. They hurried along in a black cloud of sorrow, gripped by fear and questions and concern — Mary Magdalene, Mary the Mother of James, and Johanna, the wife of Cleophas.

And how we have lauded them for their part in the Gospel narrative. Again and again, we have said: "There they were, those stalwart women, loving to the end, compassionate and sacrificial to the end, faithful to the . . ." Wait a minute! Wait a minute! Let's not get carried away with our sentimental superlatives. Yes, make them loving, if you want to. Make them compassionate. Make them sacrificially devoted. But faithful? No, I'm afraid not. Not by the broadest and most charitable stretching of the facts can you make them faithful.

Here were women who knew Christ. Here were some who had the opportunity to witness his divine ministry. They had seen his power over every enemy of life. They had seen him bring plenty out of want, health and strength out of tragic illness. Mary Magdalene herself had felt his healing touch as he brought her forth from immoral, evil insanity. They had seen him bring life out of death. They had seen every promise that he made come true. He had never given them a false word, a false promise, or a false hope. We don't know exactly how many times he told them that he would rise from the dead, but in the Gospel narratives alone, there are seventeen times that he says so. And he never speaks of his death without following it with the fact that he would rise again from the dead on the third day.

And yet, DESPITE ALL OF THIS, these women were on their way to embalm a dead body. Of course, they were hurrying, but it wasn't out of any joy or anticipation. They were trying to beat the rapid deterioration of the human body in that tropical climate. Like three undertakers, they were all immersed in the details of the interment. Who would roll away the stone? What oils and spices and preservatives were the best? Certainly nothing but the best would do.

Faithful? I'm afraid not. They were completely, utterly faithLESS! The broken seal, the shattered stone, the empty tomb — all that didn't convince them. The words of the angel, the messenger of God, didn't prove *anything* to them. Even when the Risen Christ appeared to Mary Magdalene, she made a gardener out of him. "They have taken away my Lord," she said. "Please tell me where they have laid him." It was as though everything in those women was set against believing the truth. Despite all of this evidence, despite all of these glorious manifestations, it was as though, in their human, hardheaded stubbornness, they were saying: "Look, don't confuse us. We came here to embalm a body, and that is exactly what we are going to do — we are going to embalm a dead body." They couldn't even see that the message of the angel was a rebuke and a reminder, as he said: "Why are you seeking the living among the dead? Don't you remember — DON'T YOU REMEMBER? — what he said to you?"

Well, there it is, beloved, not only for them, but for all of us — the reminder and the rebuke. Why the gloom, friend? Why the tears? Why so preoccupied with the sad task of embalming life in defeat and sorrow and tragedy? After 2,000 years of the living proof of the Resurrection of Christ, his friends are still faithless. They still need the reminder and the rebuke. The account tells us that when the women finally saw Christ alive, they ran to tell others with great joy. What about us? We've seen him alive. We've seen him live on every page of human history since his Resurrection. It's there, indelibly written, and no historian in the world can erase it. The Living Christ! We have seen him live in our own lives.

Well, where's the joy? It's no wonder that C. S. Lewis, the great British theologian, when he became a Christian, finally wrote his autobiography and entitled it, *Surprised by Joy*. To Lewis, the astounding effect of the gospel, all unlooked for, was the JOY that it brought to him. And what of us? Are we surprised by joy, or are we too involved in the embalming fluids of life? Because that's what most of us are in our culture — one great embalming party. One anthropologist sums up the history of the human race by saying: "Human beings were born, they suffered for a little while, and then they died." That covers the history of all humanity.

I told a man that my son was in medical school, and he said, "Well, one good thing is, he'll never run out of business. According to the campaign propaganda that we get every week, there's always some new, incurable disease that we're all in danger of dying of, and people are dying of right now. The only thing he'll have to learn is to tell a patient that he seems to have a touch of the virus that seems to be going around right now. They don't know what it is, but it's a virus, and they might die from it."

Another man said to me, "You know, life is funny. You finally get old enough so your mother doesn't have to zip up your pants, and then in a very little while, you're so old that you forget to zip them up unless your wife or your children remind you."

George Bernard Shaw, in his play, *Back to Methuselah*, has Adam say: "If only I can be relieved of having to endure myself forever. If only the care of this terrible Garden would be passed on to some other gardener. I'm not strong enough to endure eternity!"

Or as the poet Swinburne put it:

From too much love of living
From hope and fear set free,
We thank with brief thanksgiving
Whatever gods there be.

That no life lives forever
That dead men rise up never
That even the weariest river
Flows somewhere safe to sea.

Life then that is short, brutish, and tragic can't find any joy in eternal life. A meaningless, joyless life here is a meaningless, joyless life there.

We start out very young in our attitudes. Dick Van Dyke tells of a young mother who was trying to comfort her daughter, after her daughter's pet cat was killed. And so the mother said, "Remember, dear, that Fluffy is up in heaven with God." And the daughter sobbed out, "But, Mommy, what does God want with an old dead cat?"

Another little four-year-old boy was taken to his grandfather's funeral. A few days later, his mother heard him say his prayers this way, "God, I guess you know what you're doing, but won't you please let Grandpa out of that box?" Well, don't blame the children. You know where they get their attitudes — right from us. Our lack of faith is reflected in them. We have to stop sometime long enough to realize that all of this concerns me. It concerns my life and my attitude toward life.

It concerns the mother who stood by her baby's crib in the hospital last night, and the physician shook his head. It concerns the wife who turned to waken her husband this morning, only to find that his shoulder was cold — dead cold. It concerns the wino whose body was picked up by the police ambulance last night and carted off to the County Morgue. It concerns a Lebanese Christian killed at the same moment by a Lebanese Christian. It concerns a British soldier picked off by an IRA sniper last night. It concerns the mangled bodies of men, women, and children that are strewn along our highways right at this moment. It concerns the little child who just died of starvation on the streets of Calcutta. It concerns *every one of us* whose loved ones lie silent in the grave.

We finally have to admit that we can't find any joy or radiance in life, unless God puts it there. I don't know where else you'd find it. If you find it someplace, let me know, will you? But certainly we can't find that in a life as it's lived here. It becomes just as one man put it to me, "one damned thing after another." And that's why, if there were no Easter, we would have to invent one.

You and I are created as rational creatures. If Christ is not risen from the dead, as St. Paul tells us, what a bunch of boobs we are! We don't have any really intelligent or rational reason to go on living. But if Christ is risen from the dead, giving us the gift of eternal life, then we should live in a kind of joyful radiance.

Back in the year A.D.125, a Greek by the name of Aristides wrote one of his friends about a new religion called Christianity. He was trying to explain the reason for its popularity and its extraordinary spreading and success, and he wrote: "You know, if any man among the Christians passes from the world, they rejoice and offer thanks as they escort his body with songs of joy, as though he were setting out from one place to another place nearby."

That's what the Chritian life ought to sound like, not like an embalming party, as it so often does. Have you noticed in our conversation today, whenever we get together at a cocktail party or anyplace else, it's kind of an organ recital? Who's dying of what, where. Someone asked the great preacher, Henry Ward Beecher, if he really believed that the dead lived. He said: "Yes, I have absolute proof. If you want it, just attend a meeting of my board of deacons."

Well, I have absolute proof that Christ is risen. How? Very simple — because I have known him. I have known him ever since I was old enough to know anyone. To me, he is everything that is written in the ancient Latin symbols around the glorified cross on the altar. Notice that each one of those three-lettered words ends in "x," the sign of the cross.

REX — Christ my King
LUX — Christ my Light

DUX — Christ my Guide
PAX — Christ my Peace

I pray that the Risen Christ may be all of these to you.

Louis H. Valbracht
LENTENTIDE, 1977

14

Life: Sacred or Stupid?

The Resurrection of Our Lord, Easter Day

TEXT: John 20:1 [T.E.V.] — Early on Sunday morning, while it was still dark.

The phrase "while it was still dark," is greatly suggestive. The darkness was not only a description of the earliness of the morning, but it was a description of all people without firm belief in the Resurrection of Christ. Without that knowledge, as St. Paul has said, "we are a bunch of miserable human beings," because we have no understanding of the eternal and sacred character of human life, and for anyone trying to live it, it is a process of stumbling along in the darkness.

At the earlier Family Service when I asked the children what had happened to Jesus Christ that we celebrated today, one little boy popped up loudly enough for the entire congregation to hear: "HE RIZ!" I am surely sure that that was more acceptable to God than the response of the disciples when the women told them that they had found the tomb empty. They called it, properly translated: "Gibberish!"

Don't tell me that it's all my imagination that you are a different looking congregation of people than I have seen during the last few weeks. It shows in your faces. It rings in your voices. It exudes from your whole personality and countenance.

And don't let the cynic chime in and say that it's just the attraction of the crowds today. I have preached on Easters in some very peculiar places and to very small congregations, but the Day of Resurrection is always the same. And don't tell me it's the spring weather and that everyone feels better and is anxious to be out on a lovely Sunday morning and so you have to come to church. The first Easter that I spent in this city, we had a blizzard on

Easter morning, but that didn't change the congregation nor the joy of the service.

And don't tell me that it's commercialization, just like any of the other of our holidays. Oh, yes, the merchant may put up his sign: "Christ has risen, but our prices have remained the same." You know, it's a strange thing that nobody, no matter how hard they have tried, has ever been able to commercialize Easter. It just doesn't lend itself to commercialization — never has, never will.

One of Ernest Poole's characters in one of his poetic novels says: "History is just news from the graveyard." Well, I'll agree with him at one point. I'll agree that all of history is shaped by the news from one graveyard, one garden outside of Jerusalem in about the year A.D. 30.

Our problem is, you see, that it's not that life doesn't have any real meaning. It's the way we are living that makes it seem stupid and irrelevant and useless and meaningless. We forget that Eternal Life is not some "pie in the sky when we die" that we're talking about, but Eternal Life is the life that you and I are living today, right here where we are now!

The best news of all the world and all the years is from that garden graveyard outside Jerusalem, with a tomb that was empty, and one who had lain there standing before all humanity for all time with the assurance: "I am the Resurrection and the Life. Whosoever believeth in me, though he were dead, yet shall he live; and whoever lives and believes in me shall never die." Easter is the Good News about the universe and about Almighty God and about myself. It proclaims that the world is not some kind of an orphan asylum. It is not a mammoth machine shop. It is not a whirling ball hurtling through endless space. It is a home, and its heart is not something that the scientists are always looking for — the source of life. The heart of it is someone. It is the breathtaking news that the love of God given to us in a Risen and Living Lord is the Ultimate power in this universe!

What is human life? Oh, we've all heard the cynics. Mark Twain said: "Life would be worth living, if you could be born at the age of eighty and gradually approach eighteen." Fred Allen said that "there is no value to anything in life, except what can be put into a coffin." Or Don Herold, who said: "Life is just a few short years, from diapers to supposed dignity to decomposition." Yes, man has said, in many clever ways — or supposedly clever — that his life was stupid and meaningless. There is only one flaw in all of this. If life is as foolish and useless as they say, then their own estimate of life is just as stupid and irrelevant and senseless, and, therefore, I have no need to take account of it, because they are fools!

A Marine and I lay in the bottom of a foxhole during an artillery barrage. He struck a match, lit his cigarette, and then held the burning match up in front of my face, and with a quick puff of his breath, blew it out. He said: "That's life, isn't it, Padre?" And I replied: "You're wrong. Remember those little trick birthday candles that we used to have, where you supposedly blow out the candle on the cake and it would be dead and smoldering? Then you would turn away for a moment, and then you would look back, and you would discover that the candle was not out at all, that it was still burning brightly. That's life, Mac, and don't ever forget it."

Or there is the story of the two garment workers in the garment section of New York that Myron Cohen likes to tell. One was a cutter and the other was a stitcher. They were working side by side, and they got to talking about vacations, and the one was saying how he was looking forward to his vacation, and the other said: "I'm not going to take a wacation dis year." He said: "Why you're not going to take a wacation dis year?" The other said: "I took a wacation last year." "You did? Where did you go? I don't remember." "I went on a safari in Efrica. I went elephant hunting." "Iss that right? Did you get an elephant?" "No, I found an elephant. He charged me, but my gun jammed, and I vas killed." "Oiving, what you talking about, you vas killed? You ain't dead. You're sitting here living." And Irving replied: "You call dis living?" And so, that's what many of us must ask: "Do you call this living?"

Eternal Life is credible to us because we believe in God as a Father. We believe that God created personality and can, and will, preserve that personality, each of us, individually, because each of us, individually, is precious to him; that we are the supreme creation of the universe. We believe that the life he gives us has meaning and purpose and value, because you and I, each one of us, is actually a child of God, and what, conceivably, could take our place with God?

The other evening, in a discussion of capital punishment that I heard on television — and I wonder why we call it "capital punishment" — that's a lying euphemism. Punishment is something that we inflict in order to improve the discipline, the life, and the behavior of the person after the punishment, so how can we call it capital *punishment?* Why not call it "State Legalized Murder," which is what it actually is? But we are too delicate to use the proper words. We don't like to face it.

In that discussion, I heard the Cardinal Archbishop of Chicago make this statement: "Throughout all of history, the quality of any nation or culture can be measured by the value that it places on a human life. For the state to kill A, because he has killed B, in the wistful and unproven hope that C, observing this, will not kill D, is absolutely immoral, illegal, illogical, and ungodly." Who ever gave the state the right to do that, to use the life of a sacred human being who belongs to God for any purpose by destroying it? The discussion came up because of the decision that had been handed down by a Texas court that executions, public executions, could be televised. Well, that would be great! That would put us right back in the Coliseum in rotten, decaying, decrepit Rome. That would be the measure of our culture —

degenerate and immoral — as the people who gathered in that Coliseum centuries ago for the fun of watching people be murdered!

Also in that discussion, a prosecuter from Georgia was asked about his state and others whose laws even allow teenagers to be executed, and the youngest executed, according to the records in the history of Georgia, was fourteen years of age, and the fact that two out of three teenagers who have been murdered by the state in this country were blacks. How do we explain that? Well, the mental giant of the law of the State of Georgia to whom that question was addressed was asked whether he didn't think that executing a child of fourteen was cutting off what might be a useful and good and productive life. That genius of jurisprudence leaned back in his easy chair and sneered: "Any young man who has committed a dastardly crime has no useful or productive life ahead of him." That's intelligent, isn't it? I wonder if that Georgia prosecutor lived such a pure, sinless, and spotless life when he was a young man that he was able to say that kind of thing.

And so it is that we who have been taught by Christ of the sacredness of any human life, no matter how apparently vile or sinful, must continue to struggle against those who would destroy it, even if they are of our states or law enforcement agencies. When did God give us the right to murder any of his children?

We are so concerned in our day about endangered species — everything from the Whooping Crane to the Bald Eagle — and we sit here and stupidly don't realize that the most endangered species on the face of the earth is homo sapiens — you and me? And our nation, and a few other hairbrained nations with us, are the ones who have made us the most endangered species on this earth, in absolute disobedience to the sacredness of human life. We are absolutely against abortion when it is used as a method of population control.

Wherever Christianity has gone, slavery has disappeared, the sweat shops of factories have disappeared, child labor has been made illegal. Wherever Christianity has gone, hospitals were erected, and the word "hospital" comes from the word "hospice," which was a place where the pilgrims on their way to the Holy Land were given care and food and shelter. We have established orphanages and child placement agencies throughout the world.

And now we are, again, going to show our estimate of the sacredness of human life, because we are going to do something that has not been done before here in Central Iowa on the scale that we plan to do it. Twenty-five Lutheran congregations of three great Lutheran bodies banded together to establish Lutheran Park, which will include every level of care when it is completed for the elderly of our state and community. We are starting off with a campaign immediately following Easter for over a half million dollars to match government funds to provide residences, hospital care, nursing home care, intermediate care for the elderly of every creed, every ethnic group, not just for Lutherans.

Our responsibility as a church family is to contribute, over three years, a third of that amount of half million dollars. We'll do it gladly, and we'll do more than that, I am sure, because this is something we believe in. We have seven hundred people in our own church family over the age of sixty-five and facing these years of uncertainty and need for care. Yes, it's perhaps a trite saying that medical science has added years to life without adding life to those years, and now we intend to do what we possibly can, beginning where the old Danes began, back in 1924, and carrying on a great program from year to year that will expand, from time to time, to show our concern for the sacredness of human life that has reached those golden years.

In John Masefield's play, *The Trial of Christ*, Procula, Pilate's wife, is deeply disturbed by the crucifixion of

Jesus. Finally, a Roman centurion, Longinus, comes to her with a message that he has found Christ's tomb empty. Procula asked him: "Do you believe that he is dead?" "No, my lady." "Then where is he?" "Loose upon the world, my lady, where neither Jew nor Roman nor Greek nor anyone else can stop his Truth and his Life." That's where the Risen Christ is now — loose in the world!

Yes, in many places, his presence causes conflict, but everyplace, his presence means hope. I know, through the Risen Christ, that my world and my life in it are real and worthwhile. I know, through Christ, that my life is of value to God. I am God's son, as you are God's child. Because Christ lives, I shall live. I know that my beloved dead are not lost. In my Father's eternal care, how could they possibly be lost?

OH, HAPPY DAY! CHRIST IS RISEN! ALLELUIA!

Fingertip Embalming

The Second Sunday of Easter

Text: John 20:25b — Unless I see in his hands the print of the nails, and place my finger in the mark of the nails, and place my hand in his side, I will not believe.

Have you ever noticed? It seems that there is always one at every party. No matter how carefully you select the guests, there is always one — the wet blanket, the killjoy, the party pooper, the spoilsport, the kind of person to whom you'd like to say: "I never forget a face, but in your case, I'm going to make an exception."

I am reminded of the mother whom I was visiting in a home and, as we visited, the sounds of the children's hilarity was coming up from the family room below. Finally, the mother got up and shouted down the stairs: "What's going on down there?" And a plaintive little voice came up: "Nothing, we're just having fun." "Well, stop it!" How typical! How typical, not only of such a situation, but of you and me.

It happens every Easter celebration. It happened at the first one. At the height of the hallelujahs, they are suddenly stifled. The sweet sounds of victory go sour. It is as though someone had turned off the stereo in the midst of the "Hallelujah Chorus," and the tempo begins to slow, and the tone begins to sag and droop, and finally the whole thing sobs off into silence. And so it was on the evening of the first Easter Day. We met the wet blanket. This has customarily been the Sunday upon which we chastised Thomas, the doubter, as you heard the Gospel read. But let's look at him this morning sympathetically, with understanding, as a miserable, unhappy, and lonely figure. Surely we can identify with him.

You will notice that, in our liturgical year, this is not as it has been for years, the First Sunday after Easter. It is the Second Sunday OF Easter, and we will have a week of Easter Sundays in these seven Sundays.

But you know the feeling. You're at a party, and everyone else is having a ball. They are gay and lighthearted. They laugh and they frolic, but you aren't with the group. Your heart is weighed down by some secret sadness or depression or disappointment, so that every sound of their laughter somehow cuts through you. Every evidence of their lightheartedness and gaiety seems to alienate them from you. Even though they are your best friends, you feel like you are among strangers. Suddenly, you almost hate them for their happiness.

And so we see Thomas. The ten disciples had seen the Risen Lord. Their joy is full. All fear, all doubt, all defeat has been swept away, and you can literally see them swooping down on Thomas, shouting in their happy exuberance: "Thomas, we have seen the Lord!" And Thomas looks around at them with utter lack of comprehension. For him, Christ, and everything that he believed in and looked for, was dead. His despair was complete. And now, this bunch of madmen! In his misery and loneliness, he feels like a rejected outsider, and so he lashes out in bitterness and doubt: "So, you've seen the Lord? Great! I'll believe that when I see him myself, when I stick my finger into the scars in his hands and thrust my hand into his side."

Can you sense his misery? His loneliness? His complete estrangement from his friends? We can only vaguely imagine the tortures of the damned through which Thomas went in that next week until the Lord appeared to him also and gave him the evidence he wanted: "Go ahead, Thomas, stick your finger in the scar. Plunge your hand into my side."

And so our hearts go out to Thomas, and all who share his skepticism and doubt. We have to understand that he was rejecting — and he knew it — not only his friends, but he was rejecting life. He was doing away with the only possibility of making any sense out of human existence.

John makes it eminently clear as he says: "He who believes in the Risen Christ has life. He who does not believe is dead already." And that includes all the supposedly happy pagans who live around you — your neighbors, your friends. They seem to be doing perfectly all right without God, don't they? They're happy! They're satisfied with their lot in life. They've got everything they want. Don't be misled. They are wearing a mask, and deep in their consciousness, which they won't allow to surface, is the knowledge that they are frauds.

I remember one young man with whom I debated, trying to break through the wall of counterfeit — they're always counterfeit — intellectual difficulties that he was having with accepting Christ as Lord and Savior. "Pastor," he said, "I wish I could believe as you believe. But I can't, I just can't." I asked, "Is it that you can't believe or that you won't believe?" "Maybe that's it," he said in candor. "I know that I'm making life harder for myself, but, somehow, I just can't help doing it." And he plunged out of my study into the night and what I learned later was tragedy, unhappiness, and defeat.

Genuine doubt, you see, is doubt in our own faith. We will not to believe what we believe. I don't care whether it's Thomas or one who stands in the pulpit or one who sits in the pew. We will not have faith in our own faith. Genuine doubt, you see, is not just some kind of intellectual difficulty. It is fear — a ghastly fear — that futility and despair and death are the last words of this world.

David Hume, to whom we point as the father of the modern Age of Doubt in philosophy in the middle of the 18th Century, admitted, late in life, that he was sorry that he ever doubted, when he saw the happiness of pious, believing people. You know, I've never met an atheist. I'd like someone to bring one around some time. In thirty years, I never met an atheist. But an atheist, strangely enough, must define himself by the way of theism. He must use God to explain his own disbelief. So often he is like the man who says: "Thank God, I'm an atheist." Or as St. Augustine wisely put it: "He who rejects God has already postulated the God whom he rejects." It can't be done otherwise. It's perfectly obvious.

The lad in my Marine regiment who professed no belief in anything gave himself away when, in the heat of battle, he threw himself on a hand grenade that dropped into his foxhole to save the life of his buddy who was in the same foxhole. He did it automatically, without thinking. Why? His Christ-like belief in sacrifice, even of life, for human love, was there all the while. It sent him to his grave in a burst of faith.

Thomas, however, wanted scientific proof, but there are no such proofs, not in the strict, scientific sense, because man is both the subject and the object. He is the tester and the tested. Don't ever talk to me about purely objective science or a purely objective scientist. Poppycock! There is no such thing! he doesn't exist! The term itself is sheer nonsense. How can a scientist be objective? What does he do, jump out of his creaturehood, his personhood, to thereby make himself immune to subjective interpretation of that which he observes? It can't be done.

One scientist says: "The world picture of the Nuclear Age does not include God. The cultivated man today finds no God in his reactor. God is not among the rushing electrons, and he is not visible in outer space." This is the serpent in the garden again, whispering to Adam and Eve: "You will be as God." But, like all of the other gods of our generation, science doesn't satisfy the deep longings of the human soul. The more a man knows, the more he is aware that he knows nothing.

I'm amused. Right in this moment in our history in this country, we have all of the best economists, financiers, business leaders, and everyone working on the problem, and not one of them can tell how we can check inflation without bringing on depression. Oh, we're smart people! But put the whole kit and caboodle together, and they can't give you a rational answer.

A Harvard University student asks: "Why are we spending billions trying to create life or find the source of life, when our number one problem is to make sense out of the life that we have?" It's a good question.

Dr. Fred A. Klooster says: "True, man has come to a more realistic awareness of himself, but this experience merely shadowed his old myths and left him in skepticism and despair."

Modern writers mirror the pessimism of our times. Many have thrown up their hands and said: "There is no answer to man's dilemma." Ernest Hemingway, in *Death in the Afternoon*, says: "There is no remedy for anything in life ... death is a sovereign remedy for all misfortunes." And, of course, he proved that by committing suicide.

Eugene O'Neill, in *Long Day's Journey into Night*, typifies our philosophical attitude that life is a search for the meaning of life, and he writes: "Life's only meaning is death, so face it with courage, or even love of the inevitable. Death comes like a blanket on a cold night." And O'Neill was a damned liar when he wrote those words, and he knew it.

Arthur Miller's *After the Fall* is the story of the hopelessness of existence. Well, that's a sample of the empty, searching man.

Dr. Carl F. H. Henry said in his book, *The Nature of Man:* "While Nietzsche asserted in the 19th Century that God had died, some now add that in the 20th Century man died. Since the relationship between God and man is so close, when faith in God fades, then man's knowledge of himself is also impossible." I dare any one of you sitting here to step into this pulpit and explain who you are without reference to God or a Creator of some kind. You can't do it! Eight days after Easter, Thomas got his scientific proof. The Risen Christ stood before him and said: "O.K., Thomas, stick in your finger; thrust in your hand." And all Thomas could say was: "My Lord and my God!"

May I assure you that I do not teach religion. My faith is not in God as a Supreme Being, the Cosmic Urge, the Creative Power, the Grand Architect of the Universe, the First Cause, the Infinite Intellect — those are all phrases that we use to get out of talking about God. I know nothing about him! I believe in and preach the Crucified, Risen, and Living Christ! O, yes, we can say that the story of the Resurrection means simply that the teachings of Jesus will go on and not die. They will be like the plays of Shakespeare or the music of Beethoven, that their wisdom, truth, and beauty will never die. They will live forever. And so Christ lives.

Or, we can say that the spirit of Jesus is undying and that he lives among us as, for instance, Socrates, in the good that he left behind him and the great lives that follow his example. Or, we can say that the Resurrection is a folk tale made by confused people and is more symbolic than literal.

Hogwash!

Notice: All of these explanations are inadequate. They are simply not true because there is no account of the Resurrection in the New Testament. There is absolutely no account of the Resurrection. There is no description of what happened. Instead, it is a simple proclamation of fact: Christ is Risen! The very existence of the New Testament is proof of that. It wasn't written until forty years after. Unless something very real indeed took place on that strange, confused Sunday morning, there would be no New Testament, no church, no Christianity, no faith. As our Gospel Lesson ended this morning: "These things were written that you might believe that Jesus is the Christ, the Son of God, and that in believing, you might have life." That's the only purpose of the Bible.

In Ingmar Bergman's play, *The Seventh Seal*, he pictures a knight returning from the Crusades, with the same sense of hopelessness and futility that attended all of those Crusades, because there has never been a more stupid chapter in history than the Crusades, and when he returns, he finds the land under the scourge of the plague. And suddenly, he discovers that he has the plague, and so he bargains for some time that he might do something worthwhile before he dies. He stops at a wayside chapel along the way to make his confession to the priest. Here is part of what he says: "Is it so cruelly inconceivable to grasp God with the senses? Why should he hide himself in the mist of half-spoken promises and unseen miracles? How can we have faith in all of this when we do not have faith in ourselves? What is going to happen to those of us who want to believe, but can't? And what is going to happen to those who neither want to nor are capable of believing? Why can't I kill God within me? Why does he live on in this painful humiliation, even though I curse him and I want to tear him out of my heart? Why, in spite of everything, is he the baffling reality that I can't shake off?"

Who is the knight? You are! So am I! You know, we cannot divide the world into skeptics and unbelievers. We have to divide every individual person among us into believers and doubters or skeptics and unbelievers.

You know, at this moment, I cannot be sure, and I cannot prove, that you are sitting there. There's no way I can prove this, absolutely no scientific way that I can prove that you are sitting there. But there is one thing that I know without a shadow of a doubt, that the Risen Christ, living, is with me.

Tomorrow I may be talking like the knight. But this is an honest statement. It points out the struggle that you and I will go through until the day we die. But there is always that gift that God calls forth in us in his Holy Spirit — our faith! And I know, and perhaps you know, or you should, that the only way you can fill that emptiness in your life is fall down before him, the Risen Christ, and say "My Lord and my God!"

Embalmed With Cardiac Arrest

The Third Sunday of Easter

TEXT: Luke 24:25 — And he said to them, "O foolish men, and slow of heart to believe all that the prophets have spoken!"

I always wonder what an agnostic or an unbeliever or a skeptic does on Easter Day. Have you ever wondered that? Out of curiosity, let's join two of them on the first Easter day. For them, the story was all over, the last curtain was rung down. Their hopes lay shattered. Their dreams lay twisted and ruined. Easter Day found them on the way back home to Emmaus, back to the old home town, about seven miles from Jerusalem, back to the workaday world, back to the dull, monotonous business of eking out an existence in a dead and dying world. These two men moved in a cloud of perplexity and disillusionment. Only a week before, the Kingdom of the Messiah was riding the crest of a wave of popularity. Jesus was acclaimed with enthusiasm wherever he went. And now, the Master was dead; the collapse of the Kingdom was complete. Instead of the long hoped for triumph, there was nothing except this ignominious defeat.

And so these two men groveled along in utter despair. But let's not be too hard on them; let's not be too critical. They were too close to the horror of Calvary, too close to the cross and the debris of their own shattered hopes to see clearly. Yes, too blinded by grief to see the stranger who had joined them and was walking with them. "What was this you have been discussing?" the stranger asked. One of the disciples answered with abruptness, irritation, and exasperation: "Are you the only one of the pilgrims to Jerusalem who didn't know what happened? Jesus, the Prophet of Nazareth, was crucified, he whom we hoped would redeem Israel. And, on top of that, some of the women in our company went to the tomb this morning and came back with the report that the tomb was empty. Our men went out and found the tomb empty, as they said, but they didn't see Jesus. The women said something about seeing a vision of angels who said that Jesus was alive, but we think that the whole thing is an idle tale." And then the sad rebuke from the stranger: "O foolish men, O, foolish men, and slow of heart to believe."

Slow of heart to believe. These two men on that road to Emmaus on that first Easter became the vanguard of a great company of people, a great multitude groveling along hopelessly on the roads to their Emmauses, perplexed, despairing, disillusioned — because they will not believe what they have heard. They have, as John puts it, "made God a liar, because they will not believe what God has said."

The Risen Christ is walking with them. His words are ringing in their ears. He is here; and yet, to them, because they have closed their minds, he is dead! Dead! Even in front of them, he's a stranger whom they do not know. Why will they *not* believe? They're good, solid, no nonsense, meat and potatoes, practical men, the pragmatic, "I'm from Missouri" type. They want proof. All right, what kind? What kind will be solid enough to stick to the ribs of their minds?

There are certain laws of evidence that hold in establishing historical events. There must be documentation of the fact made by reliable, contemporary witnesses. And then, there must be effects on the other events in history that indicate that the event in question did actually occur. All right. Those are the rules. There is more reliable, documented evidence that Jesus Christ rose from the dead than there is that Julius Caesar ever lived, or that Alexander the Great died at the age of 33, that Columbus discovered America, or that Abraham Lincoln wrote the Gettysburg

Address. There is more direct, absolutely infallible evidence for the fact of the resurrection of Jesus Christ than for any of the other so-called historical events.

Isn't it strange that the historians will accept thousands of facts for which they have only the thinnest shreds of evidence, but in the face of *overwhelming* evidence of the Resurrection of Christ, they cast a skeptical eye and have intellectual doubts? Our scholars themselves set up the rules for the establishment of historical truth, and then they don't have the intellectual honesty to follow their own rules. They are like the archeologist who was chiseling away frantically at the heiroglyphics on the inside of an Egyptian tomb. One of his colleagues saw him and asked what he was doing. He said: "I'm changing this inscription so it will fit with my theories."

All right. You want the facts? In the entire history of the ancient world, there is no event that is better attested to than the Resurrection of Jesus Christ. It is recorded in overwhelming detail in all four of the Gospels, and the four that we have in our Bibles are only a minute percentage of the Gospels that were written. And these men were historians themselves, eyewitnesses who gathered the eyewitness of other eyewitnesses. It is affirmed in twenty-three out of the twenty-seven books of the New Testament by some ten different authors. It's the keystone of the faith of the early church. In fact, there is absolutely no way, historically, to explain the existence of the early Christian church, without the fact of the Resurrection. It is the reason, historically, for Easter being the crowning event of the Christian year of 2,000 years. It is the fact that caused the changing of the holy day of the week from Saturday to Sunday.

Occasionally someone will greet me with the rather trite and redundant quip: "Well, Pastor, what do you know for sure?" Common, hackneyed, and repetitive as it is, that question never fails to jar me a bit. I'm always forced to ask myself: "What do I know for sure?" and the answer always seems to be a kind of mocking echo in my mind: "Not much, and that's for sure!"

Look in God's Word for sureness, and you find a typical example. Some of the disciples were turning away from the hard sayings of Christ, and he spoke to the chosen twelve, asking, "Will you also leave me?" And Peter, as was customary, replied, "Lord, to whom shall we go? You have the words of eternal life, for we know and we are sure that you are the Christ, the Son of God." That sounds like a great affirmaton, doesn't it? Here was the confession of a man who was really sure about something. And yet, a few days later, he denied publicly that he even knew Jesus.

"The Tentative Age" is what we have been called. We haven't made up our minds. We aren't really sure about anything. The only certainty to which we cling is the certainty of *un*certainty. We are tentative, but we are also cynical and doubtful and disillusioned and skeptical. Again and again, we have found that our idols have feet of clay. A straight line is not necessarily the shortest distance between two points. And so, we find that our axioms are not axioms at all. The inflexible laws of science, we find, are not inflexible, and, therefore, they are not laws. Another telling influence of our era is our scientism — our naively worshipful attitude toward the latest pontifications of contemporary science.

Often I am confronted by a college student who is disturbed by the contrast between his courses in science and those in philosophy. In mathematics or physics, for instance, he gets Q.E.D. answers. And if you forget what the Q.E.D. stands for, you remember it is "quod erat demonstrandum" — "it has been demonstrated," that we put at the end of a geometric formula. But when they get to philosophy, when we discuss the origin, the meaning, and the purpose of life, it often sounds like guessing — intelligent guessing, but still ending up in speculation, surmise and conjecture, rather than any kind of provable certainty. The student wants to know whether in religious faith, in Christianity, there is an escape from this problematic, conjecturing to some solid convictions that one can really be sure about.

Well, the question deserves an answer, certainly, for all of us. But first of all, let us remind ourselves that many of the things that we like to think are provable certainties are not that at all. In our generation, Dr. Jeans and Dr. Milikan have been two major interpreters of modern science, and they have differed radically as to what is happening to the physical universe around us as a whole. Jeans thought that it was dispersing in every direction at such a prodigious rate that it might be said to be blowing up, while Milikan, on the other hand, thought that it was being inwardly recreated, and it was building up. At last, Milikan, discussing the differences between Jeans and himself, wrote: "The one thing in which we can both agree is that neither of us knows anything about it." Honest scientist!

Or take light. One would assume that physicists certainly understand light. And yet, one of them tells us that there are two different theories about light. Science isn't sure which one is correct. And he adds, rather whimsically, that we use the one on Mondays, Wednesdays, and Fridays, and the other on Tuesdays, Thursdays, and Saturdays. So, that's how sure they are. Dr. Robert Oppenheimer, one of our day's great scientists, said: "We guess tonight, and we correct our guesses in the morning."

Listen to the words of Thomas A. Edison: "We don't know the millionth part of one percent of anything." That's getting pretty small, isn't it? — millionth part of anything. "We don't know what water is," he says. We don't know what light is. We don't know what electricity is. We don't know what heat is. We don't know anything about magnetism. We have a lot of hypotheses about these things, but, remember, that's what they are — merely hypotheses.

Perhaps you heard about the woman who went to the doctor with back trouble. The doctor diagnosed her problem. It was perfectly obvious that her back was bothering her because she was wearing too tight a girdle. So, for the next two weeks, she went without a girdle. She went back for her next appointment, and the doctor said: "It's obvious that your back needs support. What you need to do is wear a tight girdle." And she said: "But, Doctor, two weeks ago, you told me exactly the opposite." And without any perturbation at all and completely undaunted, as physicians are in such a case, he said, "But, Madam, in those two weeks, science has made great strides."

Like the professor in the medical school who went into a drug store and asked for some monocidicacidester of salicylic acid, and the pharmacist said: "Oh, you want some aspirin." He said: "That's right, I can never remember that name."

Every week, I am told in the news that a certain kind of salad oil, or shoe polish, or soup has caused cancer in rats. Well, now, it's only a relatively few people who ever called me a rat, and so I don't know whether I should stop using these items or not. It is these differences that cause many people to ask: "Of what can I be sure?"

Certainly our first difficulty is that most of us start out with the mistaken assumption that there is only one roadway to truth — the scientific method. You see, that's what Thomas in the Gospel wanted to use — the scientific method. What is it? Demonstrable experimentation. He wanted to stick his fingers into the holes of Jesus' hands and thrust his hand into his side. This was the only way anything could be proved to him. In other words, scientific proof. That's what it is, observable evidence. And so, that's where we make our first mistake. Science is a roadway to truth, but it is only one roadway — not the only one.

For instance, I know that Beethoven's Fifth Symphony is tremendously beautiful and inspiring. I know this with an absolute and final certainty that nothing can change. If I live to be as old as Methuselah and see endless changes in scientific conclusions, even see some of Einstein's theories exploded, or perhaps hear that the American Dental Association has found that Crest tooth paste does not prevent cavities the way they thought, I will never change my mind about the beauty or the inspiration of Beethoven's Fifth Symphony. That conviction is not irrational at all, is it? It is not antiscientific, because I am not antiscientific. But, obviously, it was not science that led me to that truth of which I am sure.

For many years, I have been in love with the same woman. I didn't need any scientific aptitude test to make me fall in love with her. We filled out no psychological questionnaires. We had no genetic examinations. Our basic characteristics and personality traits were not run through any computer. She was not chosen by an IBM selector system. Frankly, I didn't fall in love with her mind. I think it was her pretty finger that pulled the trigger. And yet, this love is the most important single fact in my life here on earth. And love is not just an emotion. It is the most important method of cognition of knowing something. We never know a person until we love that person.

Amelia Burr wrote to someone she loved:

I'm not sure the earth is round
Nor that the sky is really blue.
The tale of why the apples fall
May or may not be true.
I do not know what makes the tides
Nor what tomorrow's world may do,
But I have certainty enough
For I am sure of you.

What are we saying? That there are many ways of arriving at certainty. Scientific proof is one. Oh, yes, Thomas stuck his fingers in the scars and then he fell down and said: "My Lord and my God," and Jesus rebuked him, because he had made it necessary to follow that way of the search for truth. "You've seen, you've had it demonstrated, so you believe. But happy are those who won't have your opportunity and will yet believe." Certainly, science is not the only way of finding truth.

Our daughter was once a volunteer in a summer day camp for the blind. And through her, we found out a great deal about the lives, the habits, and a greater understanding about the blind. For instance, they know that the sky is blue and that trees are green, but they still don't know what the sky or the trees really look like, because they haven't experienced them. And yet, one young blind man who visited our home said when he left: "It was good to see you, and I hope I shall see you again." He was not resorting to wishful thinking. He was stating a vital truth. The most important things in life are not known or learned by scientific observation, but by experiencing them.

How do I know what anger is? When I get angry. How do I know what love is? When I love. How do I know what fear is? When I'm afraid. One of the great errors of our day, especially among the so-called eggheads, is that truth comes through the mating of intelligence with fact, and yet, areas where we can find truth by the intellect alone are so few and so unimportant in life as to be virtually negligible. We talk pompously at times about using our intelligence to deal with the facts objectively. I always laugh when I hear that remark. There is no one in the world who ever deals with facts objectively, and the moment he says he's going to deal with the facts objectively, it has already become subjective, because he's dealing with them.

The brilliant scientist, Dr. Alexis Carrell, has said: "Intelligence is useless to those who possess nothing else. A pure intellectual is an incomplete human being. He is unhappy — terribly unhappy — because he cannot enter into the world that he supposedly knows so much about."

All right, let's look at religious truth and certainty. Certainly science itself makes God a probability. For instance, the possible contention that the universe was not created by God but arose by chance out of nothing and formed itself by accident. Dr. Frank Allen, the biochemist of Cornell University, says of this theory: "It is too absurd to deserve consideration." Yes, even science makes God a probability. But how can we change this probability into certainty? Here we might quote the great philosopher, Kierkegaard: "Existence must be content with a fighting certainty. We must remember that we are dealing with an attempted explanation of an infinite cosmos with a finite mind." And it can't be done.

Multitudes of history's noblest souls have had that "fighting certainty about God." They had their days of uncertainty, just like Luther, who said: "Some days I believe, and some days I doubt." But underneath, there is the sureness, like Paul's: "I know whom I have trusted." The basis of that assurance is that same basis that supports most of the important certainties of life — not theory, but experience. Think of some of them.

The Experience of wonder: A few years ago, we stood on the heights of the snow-covered Alps in Switzerland, and I experienced the overwhelming wonder of God's handiwork. And no one, at that moment, had to prove to me that it was his handiwork. I knew, because I experienced it.

Think of the experience of vocation: Why are people called to certain tasks, tasks that they never thought of undertaking, that they objected to, even abhorred? Until I was a sophomore in college, I was absolutely certain that I would never be so stupid as to spend my life in the ministry! Here I am. Experience, because I experienced the sense of vocation.

The experience of prayer as communion with God: Centuries of Christian living bear witness to this — the ability to say: "I am not alone. Even when I am alone, my Father is with me." As Emerson has put it: "God enters a private door to you, and you know it." God enters into every individual. And, as we pray, we are assured that we are not talking to thin air. We are in conversation with the eternal Father in heaven. Of course, no proof is possible, but then, no proof is necessary.

What do I know for sure? Well, the list isn't very long. But all the important things I know. I know not by sight, not by induction or deduction. I know by faith, by experience. I know because I am sure. I am certain, because I know. Does that sound like double talk? It isn't. This is the truth for all of us.

Think of how limited Helen Keller was in obtaining provable certainties. She could not hear. She could not see. She could not speak. When, finally, they developed that system of communicating with her, they felt the time had come that she should be told about God, and so they did. When they had finished their communication to her, she smiled and said: "I knew that God existed all the time. I just didn't know what you called him." That is what I know, for sure!

A college student said this last Easter: "Wouldn't it be terrible, after all this celebration, all of this hullabaloo, all of our songs of faith and our alleluias, if it were not true? And I said: "Yes, it would be tragic. But you know it is true, and I know it is true that Jesus Christ rose from the dead by the glory of the Father, that even Job, in the midst of his misery, his deprivation, his loss, and the stupid explanations of his friends, was able to cry out: 'I know that my Redeemer liveth'"

I KNOW THAT FOR SURE!

Embalmed Leaders

The Fourth Sunday of Easter

TEXT: John 10:14-15 — "I am the good shepherd: I know my own and my own know me, as the Father knows me and I know the Father; and I lay down my life for the sheep."

In the best tradition of science fiction, it is always a little, three-toed, one-eyed, green skinned creature with a radio antenna sticking out of the top of his skull that steps out of a flying saucer space ship and says to the first American he meets: "Take me to your leader." Have you ever asked yourself, if you were confronted by such a question, just where or to whom would you take this visitor from another planet? I suspect that many of us would be forced to answer: "I'd be glad to take you to our leader, if I only knew who our leader was myself."

May first is the anniversary of the Communist Revolution, and throughout the Communist world, the theme of the revolution is reiterated again and again, as it has been for the past sixty years: "Workers of the world unite. You have nothing to lose but your chains." Again and again, throughout the Communist world, the International will be sung:

Rise ye prisoners of starvation,
Rise ye wretched of the earth,
For justice thunders condemnation,
A better world's at birth.

And so, the revolution continues. Wherever we look on this embattled globe of ours, we see men repudiating or, at least, questioning their leadership. It would well seem that every place where we, as a nation, are involved, it is a question of leadership.

Every four years, we are treated to our quadrennial

spectacle of the National Party Convention, and as the candidates jockey for position in preparation for those events, one is driven almost to the attitude of one citizen who is asked his opinion about the two candidates for mayor of his town. He replied: "Well, all I can say is I'm grateful that only one of them can be elected."

Paul O'Neil, in a long-past issue of *Life* magazine, called the conventions "Nomination by Rain Dance," and he wrote: "No American institutions so fascinate and so appall the citizenry of the Republic (and so absolutely flabbergast foreigners) than do those vulgar, those quarrelsome, those unspeakably chaotic rites. No other such convocations, anywhere in the civilized world, perform their functions amid such torrents of hoarse, lamentable oratory, such displays of hypocritical bedlam, and such barefaced recourse to the mores of the poker table and the flea market. They are motivated by the arrant opportunism, and are such natural incubators of bathos and low comedy that their functionaries sometimes seem to be engaged in a large-scale revival of the 19th Century burlesque."

There is guile, circumvention, subterfuge, and the various forms of the old Brooklyn Bridge sale, even so crude a manifestation as, for instance, the Voice from the Sewers which called for F.D.R.'s third term nomination. Roosevelt wanted the voters to consider him the helpless victim of an overwhelming public demand, and so he had the Chicago Superintendent of Sewers down in a lower basement of the Convention Hall, with a microphone attached to the public address system of the convention, and, very obediently, the Superintendent of Sewers cried out: "We want Roosevelt" for twenty-two minutes, until a spontaneous demonstration erupted on the floor of the convention. And all of this was considered as perfectly proper in the stuggle for the power of leadership.

One can scarcely accept the excuse of the candidate who said: "I know that the office should seek the man, but I gave it plenty of time and it was apparently bashful." One remembers, rather, the opinion of Adlai Stevenson that when a man has finally gotten himself elected to public office, he is no longer fit to serve in it.

If during this period of the year in the midst of all of this power contest, you share my bewilderment, if you are a bit nauseated by the climbing, clawing clamor for leadership which goes on all around us, then perhaps you, like me, seek some kind of a relief. Like the officials of Vassar College who, when they were receiving student applications for admission, sent out the usual questionnaire to the father of one young lady who had applied, and one of the questions of the questionnaire was: "Do you consider your daughter a leader?" The meticulously honest father wrote back and in that place put: "I have never seen my daughter assume the role of a leader. However, I think she is an excellent follower." He immediately received a letter from Vassar which read: "As our freshmen class for next fall is apparently made up of several hundred leaders, we congratulate ourselves that your daughter will also be a member of the class, and thus, we are assured of at least one follower. Her application is accepted with enthusiasm and joy."

Or perhaps you seek relief in hearing from one whose claim to authority cannot be discounted or disputed, one who speaks with complete, serene, and absolute leadership. Here is one of the great "I am" statements of Jesus Christ. We have heard others: "I am the Light of the world;" "I am the vine, ye are the branches;" "I am the Way, the Truth, and the Life;" "Before Abraham was, I am;" "I am the Bread of Life;" "I am the Resurrection and the Life;" and now this, a statement that sets Christ completely apart from all others in the world: *"I am the good shepherd!"*

But I wonder if you share my confusion? After reading all of the news reports, I find myself a bit bewildered as to just who is on what side, fighting for whom and to restore what or to retain what leadership. Just who *is* in charge? No one seems quite to know. In many of the new nations of Africa with which we must deal in the United Nations, there seems to be an almost daily change of government, as one leader is overthrown and another government takes over. And we might ask ourselves if we are any better off in this free land of ours. Certainly we have, at least, cause to question it. We thought that this was a government *by* the people, but each day brings us a new and frightening sense of being crushed by a monster of our own creation.

Turn to Foreign Aid. In the twenty years from 1945 to 1965, this country spent the staggering total of one hundred and ten billions of dollars. There were twenty-two Federal Agencies engaged in the disbursing of these Foreign Aid funds, and the total for the fiscal year beginning 1966 was about seven billion dollars a year. Has this enormous expenditure accomplished its purpose? Has it halted Communism? Has it won us friends and allies throughout the world? The truth seems to be precisely the opposite.

A shrewd Latin-American commentator of Buenos Aires wrote some time ago: "There is no more pitiful role on the world stage than that of the savior. Help and aid are everywhere received grudgingly and resentfully. The United States is increasingly experiencing the truth of this but without apprehending it. Having intervened in many countries in the supposed interest of its nationals, having extended generous aid, political and financial, the United States is the most vilified nation on the globe, simply because it proffered aid." He illustrates this by developments in Indonesia and Latin American and in Europe.

Why, then, does the Foreign Aid Program continue and even expand again? The major part of the answer is the bureaucracy which has been built up under it. There are thousands of people engaged in the distribution of Foreign Aid, and their jobs depend upon it. No program in the history of mankind has more paid lobbyists than the Foreign Aid Program. Again, leaders pretending to lead have built for themselves an empire.

And so, we become frightened at the big government that surrounds us, and rightfully so. Our next impulse, then, is to turn to State power, State's rights, close at home, where we can keep, we think, more control. And if we take a close look at that, certainly, there is nothing to inspire confidence in our leadership, simply because it is more local.

Newsweek magazine, some years ago, gave us a picture in an article entitled "The Sick State of State Legislatures." Here are some glowing examples of that kind of local state leadership: The New York State Legislature, faced with an immense budgetary problem, squandered its session in futile partisan squabbling until two weeks into the new fiscal year. They yet were not operating on a state budget. Georgia's Legislature adjourned after a spirited comedy of errors, which included just a minor clerical error which produced more seats in the House than they intended to have. Michigan's lawmakers, supposedly freed for effective work by a new state constitution, had mustered neither the will nor the wit to alleviate the State's chronic financial dilemma. And Iowa's bright-eyed legislative newcomers were just getting around to solving the school consolidation problems settled by most states back in the 1800s. In Massachusetts, the legislature lurched into public view only to raise its own pay and protest the hard-hitting Crime Commission, which reported and depicted the legislature as completely lacking in moral backbone. Well, a dozen or so of our state legislatures still have an opportunity to redeem themselves, but, for most, the story is over — and it isn't a pretty story.

Maryland's celebrated lawmakers, for example, sent themselves home from Annapolis after defaulting in a court ordered reapportionment, but not without allowing in the Upper House a last minute passage of a law about which the Senate President could ask without getting an answer from the Senate: "Does anyone know what this bill is all about?" Unanswered, the bill was passed into

law, and thus ended a wild, unproductive, seventy-day
carnival that reached its height when the Speaker, who
was successor to the ex-Speaker who was serving a jail
sentence for fraud, dissolved a drunken session of the
House of Delegates with the immortal ruling:
"Gentlemen, we just can't go on this way."

This is our leadership? These are the good shepherds
upon whom we are to depend? The shepherds of the
American nation or the states? And in all of this raucous
clamor, in all of this strident, unintelligible shouting, who
can hear the quiet and insistent and eternal words of him
who stands before us and says: "I am the good shepherd.
The good shepherd giveth his life for the sheep." He
speaks of the imitation shepherds of the hirelings, the
man who is in business or leadership only for the pay,
only for what he gets out. When trouble looms, the
hireling flees. Why? Because he doesn't care for the
sheep.

Why the world revolt against its own leadership? The
heart of it is there. Men have lived peaceably under
almost every kind of rule, under kings whom they
believed served by divine right, under every kind of
totalitarian dictator, under elected presidents and
elected prime ministers, under generals, under
emperors. They accepted that leadership, the leadership
of those shepherds, just as long as they believed that the
shepherd cared for the sheep. There is an insistent need
in the human heart to know that the person who leads us
loves us — the person who leads us loves us — and the
moment we become convinced that this is *not* the case,
that he is not interested in our welfare, our safety, our
advancement toward the abundant life, the moment a
man appears to be interested only in the gratification of
his own lust for power or prestige or profit, then in the
eyes of the sheep, he becomes a hireling who cares not
for the sheep.

The ultimate question that we must then ask of
everyone — candidate for government, for office,
candidate for leadership in any business venture or any

social group: "Why do you want this position of leadership?" Isn't it strange? We never ask this in a political campaign: "Why do you want this office? What is your underlying motive? Is it love of the people or just 'White House fever,' as Robert Bender called it." Freud called it "the expression of the ego." Jung called it "the hunger for power." Adler called it "the desire for recognition." Dewey called it "the drive for significance." A modern psychologist has dubbed it "the drum major complex."

Is it the desire to be a servant of God's people or the desire to play God? How fine is the line of distinction. How often what we pass off as the desire to serve is only a desire to manipulate, to manage, and, in the end, to serve ourselves. We forget that while we were created to have dominion over things, we were not created to have dominion over people. No person created was created to have domination over any other person. He was created to *serve* other people — and there's a wide difference. No person was made to rule another — he was made to serve others.

A few years back, the president of one of the great railroads of this nation said: "The rights and interests of the laboring man will be protected and cared for by the Christian men to whom God has given control of the property of this country." Andrew Carnegie put this attitude even more clearly when he said one time, living in a day of financial giants: "The ascendency of these men was the survival of the fittest, upon which civilization depends; and these fittest men were called upon to administer the resources of the nation for the community, far better than the community could do for itself." Or, more recently, the former Secretary of Defense gave us a rule of thumb for the conduct of the affairs of the nation when he said: "What's good for General Motors is good for the nation."

The very fact that none of these statements sounds particularly unreasonable is an indication of just how easy it is for us to slip over the line, to assume godhood over the lives of our fellow humans. It's only a short step then to playing God in the lives of other people, to the temptation of identifying our immediate and selfish causes, no matter how good they might seem to us, with the will of the infinite God of the universe.

Henry Ward Beecher was one of the great Christian preachers of all time, but perhaps he succumbed to this temptation when, at the time of the Civil War, he said in one of his sermons: "This continent is to be cared for by the north simply because the north has been true to the cause of Christ. It will be governed by northern men, with northern ideas, and on northern Gospel." Or, Horace Bushnell echoes these words: "Our cause is God's cause. God is in everything. Every drum beat is a hymn. The cannon thunder is the voice of God."

Or, even a more descriptive attitude is a speech made by a Senator from Indiana, back in the debate for the annexation of the Philippine Islands when it was going on. He said: We Americans are trustees under God of the civilization of the world He has made us the master organizers of the world to establish a system where chaos reigns. He has made us adept in government that we may administer government among savage and senile people, and of all of our race, he has marked the American people as his chosen nation to finally lead in the regeneration of the world. This is the divine mission of America, and it holds for us all the profit, all the glory, all the happiness possible to man. We are trustees of the world's progress and guardians of its righteous peace." This was said a good many years ago, but it could have been said yesterday. And many of the people of our nation would agree with this attitude; but this is the very attitude of which the world is sick! And I suspect that Almighty God himself is a bit sick of it.

Yes, in a very real sense, God gave us people this historic privilege of leadership. We were given the opportunity of being the shepherd, a shepherd of the world. But leadership was given, I earnestly believe, in order that we could lead the world to the one Good Shepherd. Why have we become the most hated nation on earth? Why do people fear us and, therefore, hate us? Why is our leadership repudiated in every corner of the earth, even among our allies? Because, dear friends, we have often been acting like hirelings, because men throughout the world are now convinced that we don't care for the sheep, that anything that we do, no matter how benevolent it might look on the surface, is still motivated by our own lust for profit or prestige or world power, that our only real concern is the preservation of what we like to call our "American way of life." This means being a millionare in the world when everyone else is starving, if necessary. Well, aren't they right? Let's be honest. Aren't they right? The only impression we've ever made in the world is the pitiful pittance, by comparison, that the churches of the United States have given to the peoples of the world, because this, they know, was given in love, this, they know, was given in a real spirit of service and leadership in the world.

We look today for leadership. Our government has talent scouts looking everywhere for leadership. What kind of leadership must it be? The Good Shepherd, he must be the spirit that guides all of our leadership. As one of the princes of England, just before his coronation, questioned the Prime Minister with these words: "Mr. Prime Minister, in my rule as king, I want above everything else that the people of England should be loyal to me, that they should be obedient and that they, above all else, should love me. What does it take?" The Prime Minister replied: "It takes only what you have to give — your love and your life."

"He who would be great among you, let him be your servant. He who would be chief among you, let him be your slave, even as the Son of Man came not to be served but to serve and to give his life, for the Good Shepherd giveth his life for the sheep."

Embalmed Alive

The Fifth Sunday of Easter

TEXT: *John 14:6 — Jesus said to him, "I am the way, and the truth, and the life; no one comes to the Father, but by me."*

The words are probably the most plain, the most authoritarian, the most all-inclusive of the great "I am" statements made by Jesus Christ. In the 14th Chapter of the Gospel According to St. John, the 6th verse: "I am the way, the truth, and the life." In unmistakable, explicit words, our Lord is saying that the human being cannot have life without him. I suppose that our culture can be divided into two types of persons — those who say in whatever comfortable and luxurious situations they find themselves in: "This is the life!" And the other group who looks around them in frustration, bewilderment, and a plaguing sense of uselessness and asks: "What's life all about, anyway?"

A periodical tells us a story about the last days of the late actor, John Barrymore. That incorrigible character was confined to his bed most of that time with a serious illness. His instructions from his physician were quite clear and simple. He could have very little to eat, very little to drink, very little exercise, and very little visitation from his friends. One evening his nurse had brought him his crumb-like meal, and as she gave it to him she asked him if there was anything else he would like. He said: "Yes, would you please bring me a postage stamp. I'd like to do a little reading."

I'm sure that many of us know lives all around us which are lived on just about that plane, lives that have never gotten beyond a little bit of this and a little dab of that, certainly lives that never reached the dimensions or the stature that God intended for them. Pinched and cramped and jammed into a little space, they are eked out in an almost kind of solitary confinement. There are those whose lives have never reached beyond the outward shell of their own skins, lives that are bound up completely with their own physical welfare and comfort and health. Certainly, we all know lives of this description, the person who goes around with one burning concern in life: "How do I feel? How do I feel? Is my motor running smoothly? Is my plumbing operating efficiently? That little pain that I felt, is it better or is it worse?"

Conversation at social gatherings, for many of us, continues to be an organ recital, the deliciously gory details of some recent surgery that someone had, something that the doctor told me about myself, that fascinating travelogue "Inside John Doe or Mary Jones," the magazine article that I just read — and you can't pick up one without finding some medical title in the Table of Contents. But did you ever sit back and quietly observe such a conversation? Actually, not one person is the least bit interested in the insides of any other. Each waits with rather ill-concealed impatience until someone has barely finished the discussion of his symptoms so he can plunge in abruptly to tell about his own. His is the case that is really important, interesting, and significant in this game of organic one-upmanship. Even one of our presidents felt moved to publicly display and have photographed his gall bladder incision.

For many, if life goes at all beyond the inside of the body, it is only bounded by what directly concerns the body — its comfort, its pleasures, its satisfactions, its decoration. Our ridiculous preoccupation with cosmetics, clothes, or fashions, whether my pants are properly pressed or whether a lady's skirt is short enough to show her bottom when she sits down becomes a matter of vital concern in life, doesn't it? We don't need any slim tailoring or tight girdles to make us look small. We are small, with little lives.

Some lives never get beyond the house or the job. Our homes may be our castles, but for many of us, they become prisons. We don't live in our houses, we live for them. Or our jobs, whatever they may be, require our whole concern. We proudly inform one another that we are keeping our noses to the grindstone. Well, it's fairly safe to assume that if you live life in that position, you won't see anything except the grindstone. What a pitiful picture we are, laboring and sweating and striving for things which we think make up our living. We jam ourselves together into little buses, little cars, little airplanes, little elevators. We crawl through dark canyons filled with smoke and soot and exhaust fumes. We worm our way into that little place where we do our job. We work out our hours there, and then we go home to sit in the middle of a little piece of real estate. And this is our life! Do you have for one minute the insane notion that this is what Almighty God meant for your life to be, he who created you in his image?

In the 6th Chapter of 2 Corinthians, Paul lists for us some of the prime paradoxes of the Christian life. You remember the list: Poor, yet rich; sorrowful, yet rejoicing; unknown, yet well-known; and so on. There is one in that list that is intriguing. He states the paradox: "Dying, yet behold, we live." But the thing that is fascinating about that paradox is that you can reverse it. You can also say it backwards, and it will be just as clearly true, as: "Living, and yet behold, we die," for this makes a tragedy out of the triumph, as we reverse it, and it is, for so many persons, tragically true, as living, and yet behold we die. What a condition!

If I should die, thus, while I am still living, think of the implications. God's will is frustrated. His loving, creative activity in bringing me into being is all brought to nothing. He has brought forth a tree, and the tree has brought forth no fruit. He has made a creature with a potential of life, love, service, and fellowship; and the thing went dead before any of these possibilities, before any of these magnificent potentials were realized. It is the searching question that our very creation demands that we answer: "Have we fulfilled the purpose of our creation, or have we died without ever having lived?"

We cannot forget the stinging parable of Christ concerning the fig tree and the vineyard. The owner of the vineyard comes seeking fruit, and he finds none. And he says to the husbandman of the vineyard: "For three years now, I have come to this tree seeking fruit, and each time I seek the fruit, I find none. Therefore, cut it down and cast it out. Why should it take up space any more? Why should it any more be a burden to the soil?" It's a question aimed at all of us. Our Lord asks: "What earthly good are you? What right do you have going on taking up space in the world, eating its food, breathing its air, using up its resources? Just the mere fact of being born and existing isn't excuse. It doesn't give us that right." What our Lord is saying, literally, is that each of us has the obligation of justifying the fact that he's going on living. He holds up the very real possibility that we may be dead, even though we are going through the physical motions of life.

Perhaps we may illustrate what we mean by an incident in the life of a professor who was walking on the grounds of a great European university, and one of the students was walking with him. The student had been attracted there by the reputation of the university, by the sense of prestige that that famous place gave him. He was planning to study law. "And what," said the professor, "will you do when you have finished?" "I will take my doctor's degree." "And then what?" "After several difficult cases call attention to myself by eloquence and learning, I'll gain a great reputation." "And then what?" "Well, I suppose I shall die." And then the professor turned toward him and with his thundering voice said: "AND THEN WHAT?" The young man had no answer. The last question had struck home. He realized the futility of making a livelihood and losing a life.

There are some little lines of the poet:

Living to make a livelihood, solely that,
Then times are hard, very hard.
Living to make a life, wholly that,
Then times are good, very good.

And so, we may look at many an unhappy life and discover that it is unhappy because it's no life at all. Thoreau once replied to a letter from one of his dull, conventional friends, who had written concerning his worry about his own health and the various diseases that he suspected he had contracted and what dire results they might have, and Thoreau wrote and said: "I would stop worrying about your health. I suspect you're dead already," intending to shock him out of what he knew was a lifeless kind of existence. But such persons are legion. Such dead lives are common among all of us.

What is the advice of the world, how to live?

Adjust to society;
Conform to the pattern;
Live an average life;
Don't stick your neck out or go off the deep end for anything;
Don't be too fanatical about any conviction;
Fit yourself into a little groove and stay there and be safe;
Live a reasonably moral life, at least as good as the average person;
Get an average job, and work the average number of hours, at the average amount of effort, at least as hard as the average person;
Be decent to your neighbors;
Pay your taxes;
Be a good citizen;
Be a good parent, according to PTA standards;
Support the church, attend once in a while when it's

convenient;
See that your children go to Sunday School;
Keep the dandelions out of your lawn, so the seeds
    won't blow on the lawn next door;
Carry enough insurance to pay the undertaker;
Brush your teeth twice a day, and see your
    psychiatrist twice a year;
And use Dial soap, so you'll be socially acceptable.

Very often there comes to mind a young man with whom I worked in one of America's large, industrial plants. We spent many weeks together on a labor gang. I remember him because he is so typical, a sample of a great host of the American people. From Monday morning to Friday evening, he would go through the motions of working. He would never do one with more than was demanded of him. When the opportunity offered, if the foreman was out of sight, he would lie down on the job. He grumbled and groaned all day, cursing the fate that had made him a laborer and, with equal vehemence, cursing those who through, as he said, luck or pull or dishonesty had positions above him. On Friday evening, he would seize his pay envelope and dash from the plant. And the weekends that he told me about included drunken debauchery, lewd women, the amusement park, a gambling table, a dance hall, or some girl's bedroom. And on Monday morning, he would show up again at the plant, tired, with bloodshot eyes, and borrow some money from me to buy his lunch. I asked him about those weekends: "Why? Why did he do it? What did he get out of it?" His answer was also typical: "What do you think I'm working for? A man who sweats out his guts all week in this sweatshop has a right to a little happiness on the weekends." Happiness! That was what he was laboring for, so he could be happy on the weekend. Poor, misguided soul; and yet, so typical, so common.

Or go to the other end of the economic scale. An article in *Coronet* magazine is titled "The High Price of

Success." It states: "The corporation is taking the place of the Other Woman in the so-called eternal triangle, and the staggering impact on executive marriages suggests that big business is the most demanding mistress of all. According to psychologists, physicians, family counselors, and others, companies now absorb too much time, energy, and devotion of the rising young executive. Exhausted by their jobs, they are mere shells at home, unable to function efficiently as husbands or as fathers. The result is seldom divorce, which is bad for careers of young men on the go. Instead, marriages in name only are preserved between weary, indifferent men and women beset by all sorts of emotional ills, including chronic loneliness, sexual frustration, alcoholism, and excessive dependence on their children. In some New York suburbs, counselors will tell of families composed of emotionally disturbed or delinquent children, bitterly frustrated wives, and husbands so neglectful they do not even realize what is happening to their home lives. The president of one New York firm, for example, was home only every other weekend, and he usually spent that on the golf course or in the steam room at the country club. Only after one of his teenaged children attempted suicide did he discover that his wife had become an alcoholic and another child was addicted to narcotics." This is the large, full, successful life?

Is it any wonder that thousands of our people that we termed disparagingly "Hippies" said: "I'm sorry, we will not join your stupid rat race." We were insulted and hurt, and we chastised them verbally, because no one must question this. This is the good life! Everybody says it is!

Some others do the things a little differently. They slave away monotonously for fifty weeks for that two weeks they receive as vacation. This is their reward. For two weeks, they will live! Or they slave away for years so that they can be happy and secure when they retire in old age. Watch them. See how happy they are. Go through those retirement homes. Visit those retirement communities. See the joy, the security, the largeness of life!

Do you want to look at the feminine side? I read an interview of Zsa Zsa Gabor — and that's about as feminine as you can get, I guess. She was asked why she married so often, what was she looking for? "I'm a very feminine woman," she said. "I'm looking for a man who's going to spoil a wife, and look after her, and take all her headaches away. But, so far, none of my husbands have ever done that. The type that attracts me, and I always marry, are the ones who don't want to look after a woman." She shook her head sadly. "It must be a very dull life to love only one person in a lifetime, but it also must be a very wonderful life, because you can build a life together, and you don't have to start all over again each time." Is there any hope for her? "I hope so," she laughed. "I wouldn't like to live without hope." And if she found herself in a right marriage, would she give up her career? "If I find the right man, if I can once relax, of course, I'll happily give it up," she said. Clearly, for Zsa Zsa Gabor, as for millions of women the world over, a man she can care for and who will care for her and who will give her security is all she asks of life. Is that all, ladies? Is that what you want?

Most Americans talk about happiness, and what is it, this happiness that we seek? Where and how do we find it? The search is mad and wide and varied. In the quest for happiness, one man searches the Arctic regions, one grows roses, one writes poems, one paints pictures, one becomes a monk, many become sensualists. Our night clubs, our movie theaters, our race tracks, our sports amphitheaters are filled with millions in quest of happiness, this illusive something. One man buys a dozen houses, another goes into the wilderness. In the midst of all of the search, each man has the conviction that somehow, somewhere, under certain conditions, there are things, deeds, and a way of living that can make him happy.

A noted psychiatrist asks in a *Pageant* magazine article why so many married women are having affairs today. He concludes: "Modern-day wives have been around more before marriage; they're often experienced sexually or they've read books and know what they should be getting out of their sex lives. Therefore, they're less apt to sit in the house, rear children, and tolerate an unstimulating sex life. Today it is easier for women to support themselves and to avoid pregnancy. The result is that they can afford to be realistically independent. Their attitude is: I really know what I want, and I'm not getting it with my husband. So I'll find it elsewhere." "My estimate," says the doctor, "is that one out of every five wives today sooner or later has an affair." Are they getting what they want? Not the ones that I meet day after day.

Most Americans think of happiness in terms of separate episodes and experiences — a movie, a meal, a car, a book, a trip — instead of thinking of happiness as the whole of life not dependent upon separate episodes or possessions. Therefore, we are unhappy people. All this because we are convinced that the later years of maturity stretch out as a kind of barren wasteland before us. This is tragically the natural and inevitable conclusion which must be reached when lives are lived according to our contemporary philosophy.

The French painter, Broulette, earlier in this century, depicted in a series of paintings the frustrations and defeats of contemporary life. In the first picture he shows a frantic man searching for some important piece of paper. The room is in a shambles, drawers are open, papers scattered about. Behind him is the figure of Satan holding the missing paper high above the head of the desperate searcher. This is the search for some new and enticing sensation in life. One philosopher has said that ours is the "Age of Sensation." How frantically we search for some new experience. The world beckons with them, everything from a new thrill ride on the midway of the State Fair to some new perversion of our sexual nature.

Men are searching for something that will make life better as it goes along, and the search is fruitless.

Another painting depicts a haggard man in a large field, digging with a spade. Behind him are numerous holes that he has already dug, and beside each hole is a box with the cover open; and the boxes are all empty. Here the painter is depicting an empty life, spent striving for futile and empty goals. We have worshiped the god of material progress. It has become the sacred cow of the man on the street. Our scientific and industrial discoveries will — we wistfully hope — make our lives richer, bigger, fuller, as they go along. Life will be larger for us this year because we are planning to get a color television. If only we can find the cure for the common cold, invent a new mouse trap, or own an automatic dishwasher, life is sure to be finer in our declining years. All the commercials say so, and we have to believe them. This is what we're working for! It's got to be true, hasn't it? This is what we work for! Empty boxes. We dig our holes. We open our boxes. And they're empty!

The last painting is of a man bound and gagged and tied in a chair, while his terror-stricken eyes watch a thief rob his room of all his valuables. Here is our futile attempt to find security in possessions. Placing our faith in these things, we end up only with the nagging fear that there isn't going to be enough. Look again at our aged people. Every day is the fear they won't have enough to last them, the more they have, the greater the fear. And all of the events of life keep tapping us on the shoulder and saying: "Thou fool, this night thy soul." Thou fool!

But the Word of God presents to us the truth that life need not be that way. How is something else accomplished? A story in *Newsweek* magazine some time ago tells of a middle-aged couple who had been discussing the brevity of this life as compared to the eternity after death. So they decided to give away all that they had. He entered a Roman monastery; she went into a convent. They would probably not see each other for the rest of their lives. Poor, misled souls. This is not the answer! That is not living a life — that's an escape from it, this retirement to a religious seclusion.

This is not what Christ meant when he said: "I came that ye might have life and have it more abundantly." Eternal life is not something that we prepare for in the dim distant future after death. We believe that when we accept Christ as Risen, Living Lord and Savior, we have entered into life HERE. We see life here upon earth as a part, but only a part, of that eternity. We see this brief pilgrimage in relation to the whole. In that light, life takes on new meaning, new richness. There are no declining years. Life is lived on the ascending scale. We are storing up spiritual riches. We perfect, as far as possible, the lovely art of worship. We learn to know the eternal joy of fellowship with our Eternal Father, and that association lightens and enriches our association with our fellow men. Love, joy, and deep abiding peace — these are the fruits of such a life. Oh, that we might understand that as our life grows.

Michelangelo once came into the studio of his student, Raphael. He looked at a painting that Raphael was doing as it stood there on its easel. And then, in anger, he picked up a large brush, dipped it into the paint on the palette, and across the canvas in large letters he wrote: "Amplius!" Larger! You can't deal with life, in little, cramped, weak, and indistinguishable figures, filled with fears and frustrations. Or, as the woman who visited the psychiatrist was told to go home and take the mirror down over her sink and cut a window in the wall so that she could see beyond her dirty dishes and her house and herself.

I don't care who you are, or what your name is, or what you work at, or how much you have piled up, I will tell you the eternal truth that you will not find life here within yourselves. As one modern play has it: a poor, sick man is dying, and nobody understands his malady, dying in the rat race. Finally, they operate, and they make an incision as long as his body; and they are all surprised to find nothing except hollow blackness. You can't make a life within you. You can't make a life out of this. I don't care how you dress it, or paint it, or care for it, or keep it in live and sparkling health, how you delight it, how you pleasure it, how you secure it, how you comfort it — your life can't *be* in there, friend. You'll never find it!

In the marvelous economy of our Creator when he says, through his Son, "Thou shalt love the Lord thy God with all thy heart and soul and mind and thy neighbor as thyself," he isn't giving us some arbitrary rule that we have to follow to be good, godlike children. He is giving us the essence of human life, that life has to be lived that way or it won't be lived. We have to live in God and in our fellow man. Life, to become larger, must always go outward. There is no other way that it can grow.

"I am come that ye might have life and have it more abundantly."

The Hard-to-Believe Promise

The Sixth Sunday of Easter

TEXT: John 14:13 — "Whatever you ask in my name, I will do it, that the Father may be glorified in the Son."

As our Lord took leave of his disciples, promising them the coming of the Holy Spirit and the power that would be thereby transmitted to them and through them, he repeated a promise which he had made before. He was attempting to reiterate the power that we have at our fingertips, if we only believe it. Actually, it concerns the subject of prayer, because any petition addressed to Christ is a prayer. So when he says: "Whatever you ask *in my name*, I will do it," we have the whole key to the power of prayer. The reason many of our prayers go apparently unanswered or are answered only with a negative silence is the fact that the petition is not addressed in Christ's name. The whole power of prayer depends upon that qualifying statement: "Whatever you ask in my name." If we are skeptical because God does not seem to answer our prayers, then we must ask of our petitions whether they are worthy to be asked in the name of Christ. Obviously, many, or perhaps most, of our prayers do not come under this category.

What we speak of comes under the heading of things difficult to believe, because we are speaking of the power and the efficacy. of prayer. Prayer, oh, yes, that's something that we talk about, laud, praise, in Sunday School; and then, the rest of the time, regard with a high level of skepticism and neglect. Perhaps the little girl is more truthful than we would like to believe, when she asked her mother why they always said their prayers just before going to bed. Quite understandably, she inquired: "Is it because the rates for long distance are cheaper at night?" The objects of our prayers, and the answers to them do seem like a long, long distance away.

Do you remember the incident in *Huckleberry Finn* where Mark Twain has Huck make a very human observation? "Miss Watson took me into a closet and prayed, but nothing came of it. She told me to pray every day, and whatever I asked for, I would get. But it weren't so. I tried it. Once I got a fish line but no hooks. I tried praying for hooks, three, four times, but somehow it wouldn't work. One day I asked Miss Watson to try for me, but she said I was a fool. She never told me why. I couldn't make it out in no way. So I says to myself, if a body can get anything he prays for, why don't Deacon Wynn get back the money he lost on pork? Why don't the widow get back the silver snuffbox that was stole? Why don't Miss Watson fat up a bit? No, I says to myself, there ain't nothin' to it." Yes, Huck's concept of prayer is too tragically common. Prayer, to many, is a kind of process of looking over a menu of what life has to offer and then ordering all the best things, with the full expectation that God, like an attentive waiter, will scurry around and provide them for us.

And so, again and again, we wonder about our prayers. Many of the questions are thoughtful and sincere. There's a legitimate area of confusion and questioning. The other day, I was reading the musings of one of our pastors in Buffalo, New York. He was telling of the tornado that tore through that area of the nation some years ago, you remember. It roared through Michigan and Ohio, leaving death and devastation in its wake. And then, strangely, inexplicably, it leaped over Buffalo and dipped down again to rip through Worcester, Massachusetts, and level it to the ground. That night, all through the night, people prayed, as they heard on the radio and television warnings blared out of the devastation, the impending disaster that was waiting them. Buffalo was spared. But hadn't people prayed in Flint, Michigan? Hadn't there been thousands of prayers go up from Worcester? And so, the morning after, we were left wondering. Why did the people in Buffalo live and the people in Flint die?

Again and again, I relive the scenes of the battle of Iwo Jima. Hadn't we all prayed at Iwo? I am sure that there was not a human heart in that whole island from which some prayer had not been wrenched. And yet, for years now, the grass has been green on the graves of those who died all around me. Why am I still alive? During the retreat to Dunkirk, for several days, the English Channel was whipped by storms, you remember. And yet, on those important days, when the ships and boats of every description came out to gather up the remnants of the retreating British Army and take them back across the Channel, the Channel was strangely glassy and quiet and calm. And again and again, it was said: "God did this."

You read the words of Johnny Bartok of Eddie Rickenbacker's crew, describing those days when they were forced down in the Pacific: "As soon as we were in the rafts and at the mercy of God, we knew that we were in no condition to expect help from him. We spent hours each day confessing our sins to each other and to God, and then we prayed, and God answered, and it was real. We needed water. We prayed for water. We got water. We asked for fish. We got fish. We got meat when we prayed. Sea gulls don't go around sitting on people's heads, asking to be caught. On the eleventh day, when the plane flew over, we cried like babies. It was then that I prayed to God: 'If you send that plane back, I'll tell everybody that I believe in you.' Other planes flew on, but that plane came back. Why? Did it just happen? No, God sent that plane back."

And so it is with our prayers. What do we make of all of this? More people than we can guess ask: "What does it all mean?" Whether it's grief or gladness, tears or triumph, pain or pleasure, they say: "What did I do to deserve this? Was it prayer?" Well, it's a true but tragic fact that few people really pray today. In only about thirteen percent of our homes do we even go through the perfunctory performance of saying grace before meals, and then, usually, only when children are present. Why our lack of prayer? Why our skepticism? Perhaps one college student's answer will suffice. He put it to me this way: "We don't have to pray for things today. We have the brains and power to go out and do them and get them for ourselves, without any superstitious dependence upon prayer."

Or, perhaps, we could put it this way. Many of you watched the television program "CBS Reports on Unidentified Flying Objects." The sum and substance of the whole report was that if there were UFO's around, we have the equipment and the knowledge to know that they are there and they are not. But I was particularly intrigued with the final statement of that program, made by a young, brainy, eminent astronomer. The reporter had asked him why he thought there was so much interest in so many observations of UFO's today, if they didn't really exist. And with sophisticated, intellectual snobbery, he said, with all of the country listening and as the final punch line of that program: "Oh, I suppose it's our contemporary substitute for God. They take the place of that superhuman, omniscient, all-seeing, benevolent creature out there some place that people like to think are watching over them but in which nobody believes very much today."

There it is, fellow citizens, and I shuddered, because it gives us the answer for our neglect of prayer, our obsession and our preoccupation with our own power to answer our own prayers! Power — it's the keynote of our age, power windows, power brakes, power steering, power garage doors, power politics, computerized power, transistorized power, industrial power, financial power. We are strong. We are independent. We need no help of any kind from anyone. We are wise and powerful, wealthy and affluent. Rufus Jones tells the story of the daughter of a farmer who had become very prosperous, who went into the village store. The storekeeper, trying to make friendly conversaton, asked: "And how are your hens laying? Are they laying well?" "They can," the girl replied, with her nose in the air, "but in our financial position, they don't have to."

And so, we are obsessed with our own power, our own wealth, our own affluence. I shudder, again and again, when I hear the witnesses before our Congressional Committees report that we are still capable of standing alone with our own power and fighting off the rest of the world single-handedly, if necessary. Our Lord said, prophetically, of us: "So far, you have asked nothing in my name. Ask and receive that your joy may be full." And, again and again, by word and attitude, we have said: "Please, Lord, we'd rather do it ourselves! Don't worry about us. We have the power!" Power, the keynote of our day, whether it's personal or national.

We find it very hard to understand a statement like Paul's, when he says: "When I am weak, then I am strong." In the diaries of Paul Goebbels, that fiendish voice of Nazi superman propaganda, he refers two or three times to Mahatma Gandhi. In each case, he calls him a fool and a fanatic, because he chose a course of nonresistance and peaceful revolution to seek the freedom of India. In Goebbels's estimate, only force, only power, could achieve victory in the world. It was the only thing that really had meaning." Today, Nazi Germany is just a terrible memory — and India is a growing, independent nation. That which Goebbels thought was strength was weakness. That which he thought was weakness was strength. Today our greatest danger, beloved fellow citizens and fellow Christians, is not our weakness. *Our greatest danger is our strength!*

Consider the dangers of power. When Laval asked Stalin not to antagonize the Pope, Stalin merely retorted: "How many divisions does the Pope have?" One of the dangers of power: it makes men overconfident. It blinds their eyes to reality. Samson, in the Old Testament, was supremely confident of his own strength and physical power. He had never read the modern magazine advertisement "Never Underestimate the Power of a Woman." But Delilah used his own strength against him, his power. His very strength was his weakness.

Power corrupts. Men lose their respect for human rights and human dignity. They begin to feel superior to moral law, to divine law, to human rights, to *any right*, except their own, backed up by their own invincible power. The lust for power works like termites, boring from within, leaving outside what appears to be strong but is rotten and crumbling at the core. Wasn't it Alexander the Great who became so arrogantly irritated when the terrible storm would not allow his great armies to cross the Straits of the Dardanelles that he commanded his soldiers to go out and beat the waves with rods to punish the water?

Men in their power and their prosperity lose their understanding of the power of the unseen. The unswerving steadfastness of the democracies during World War II completely mystified Hitler. He didn't know what kept them going, what held them up. How do they keep on? You see, he had forgotten the unseen power of the spiritual forces of Almighty God. And, notice, that Almighty God always works his will, not with the power of men, but with the weakness of men. Can we read history? The evidence is there. Every nation that has feverishly prepared for a war has lost it! Our nation has been unprepared for every major war into which we have been forced, and we have never lost one! Our very weakness was our strength! This nation's strength has not been in its power to destroy but in its power to construct. It has not been our alliance with armies but our alliance with God that gave us strength.

Remember the Constitution. Most of the state constitutions of this union contain statements acknowledging that that state is established with the dependence upon the power of Almighty God. The first university in this land had as its motto: "To the glory of

Christ." The framers of the Constitution of ths nation called this country "a divine adventure in a new type of Christian commonwealth." For years, the *only* book that we used in our public schools — the only book we used in the schools of this nation — was the Bible! We talk a great deal about the American way of life. Do we remember, any more, what the American way of life really is?

We are strong, when we know how dependent upon God we are. Each time we are faced with some desperate crisis, we have prayed. No, Christ doesn't explain in minute detail just how prayer works. He doesn't explain how he makes giants out of weaklings. He doesn't explain how he makes strength out of weakness. But we do know that, as a people, as a nation, we have lived by the power of prayer — Washington on his knees at Valley Forge, Lincoln confessing that when his knees shook, he knelt on them.

Remember the day after the day of infamy, December 8, 1941, when President Franklin Delano Roosevelt confronted the Joint Session of Congress and the entire nation over the air? Our Navy was at the bottom of Pearl Harbor. Our handful of troops, scattered around the world, were ready for almost immediate defeat and annihilation. We were weak, defenseless, unprepared. We could not raise a hand in our own defense. And yet, his voice came out with a ringing affirmation of victory — ultimate, inevitable victory! But, remember this, fellow citizens — oh, may we never, never, never forget it — that his last words were a prayer: "Help us, God! Help us, God!"

So may we remember the hard-to-believe promise of our Lord: "Whatever you ask in my name, I will do it, that the Father may be glorified in the Son."

The Embalmed Come Alive

The Ascension of our Lord

TEXT: Luke 24:49 — "And behold, I send the promise of my Father upon you; but stay in the city, until you are clothed with power from on high."

I was amused, if a bit sadly amused, at the cartoon that I saw in an issue of *The Lutheran* magazine. It shows a man leaping up from his pew in the middle of a worshiping congregation. He is waving his arms in the air. His mouth is open with a shout of joy and glee. And beside him, his wife is frantically trying to pull him back into his seat, and she is saying: "O.K., so you feel the Spirit, but *not here* in this Worship Service."

That's about the way it is with us, isn't it, the main line denominations outside of what we sometimes disparagingly label the "Pentecostal Sects"? We are perfectly willing to talk about God the Father, our Creator and Preserver. We certainly have a great deal to say about Jesus Christ, our Lord and Savior; but when it comes to the work and the power of the Holy Spirit, we become strangely silent. A lot of people will testify that they have finally "met the Lord," that "they have found Jesus," that "they have turned their lives over to Christ," but the Bible tells us that "no person can say that Jesus is Lord and Savior except through the power of the Holy Spirit."

A Methodist bishop once said that if the Pentecost, that tremendous coming of the Holy Spirit and birthday of Christ's Church, would recur at a National Convention of the United Methodist Church, they would probably appoint a special committee to investigate this phenomenon and report two years hence.

One of our mothers tells me that she was getting her little son costumed for Halloween Beggars' Night, and the easiest thing for her to do was to take an old sheet and cut it up and dress him as a ghost. As the process of costuming was going on, I guess the lad remembered what he had heard in the Creed during church Services, and so he asked: "Mom, will the Holy Ghost be out tonight, too?"

I ask my Confirmation Class how they know that something they are doing is either right or wrong, and they reply with the normal answer: "Well, my conscience tells me so." And I ask the obvious next question: "And what is your conscience?" And they reply, usually: "Well, my conscience is a kind of little voice inside of me that tells me what's right and wrong." And I ask the clinching queston: "Whose voice?" And then they are silent. They realize that the answers that they have given previously are really childish, nonexplanatory, if not stupid. But let me assure you that many adults are equally reluctant to answer that question, even though we say in the great Creed of the church, the Nicene Creed, which was written by the Council of Nicea, the first Council of the Church, in the year 325: "We believe in the Holy Spirit, the Lord and Giver of Life, who proceedeth from the Father and the Son, who with the Father and Son together is worshiped and glorified, who spake by the prophets."

Or in Luther's explanation of the Third Article of the Creed concerning the Holy Spirit, we dutifully recite: "I believe that I cannot by my own reason or strength believe in Jesus Christ my Lord or come to him. But the Holy Ghost has called me through the Gospel, enlightened me by his gifts and sanctified and preserved me in the true faith."

In other words, we are testifying that we have absolutely no relationship with God the Father or with Christ our Savior except through the Holy Spirit working through the Word and the Sacraments, as he does. The means — the only means — through which we can have relationship with the Father and the son is through the power of the Holy Spirit.

People will say that somehow God seems to have deserted them, that they cannot feel his presence. They never hear his voice talking to them. They are talking the same kind of hogwash as the man who said he was going to sell his waterbed because he felt that he and his wife were drifting apart. God is not drifting away from you. I assure you of that. God is there, and he is speaking through his Spirit. It is just that you aren't listening!

In George Bernard Shaw's play, *Saint Joan*, Joan hears voices from God. The king is very annoyed about this, and as Joan stands before the king, he says: "Oh, your voices! Your voices! I am the king. Why don't the voices come to me instead of you?" And Joan replies: "They do come, but you do not hear them. You have not sat in the field at evening, listening for them. Oh, yes, when the angelus rings, you cross yourself and have done with it, but if you prayed from your heart and you listened to the trilling of the bells in the air long after the bells have stopped ringing, then you would hear the voices as well as I do." Joan is a vivid example of Christian truth that ordinary men and women gain the strength of giants and the power of miracle workers when they wait on God for the empowering of his Holy Spirit. But there are a lot of you who don't believe that, do you? You really don't!

We are like the basketball coach who was questioning one of the new candidates for his team, and he was asking the boy why he wore such long hair, clear down to his shoulders. The lad replied: "I wear long hair because Jesus wore long hair." At which the coach grabbed him by the arm, led him over to the swimming pool, and said: "O.K., let's see you walk on the water." But the coach had forgotten that there was one man who did walk on the water at the bidding of Christ and by the power of the Holy Spirit! Peter walked upon the water!

Today we celebrate the Holy Spirit as it came in the Baptism of Jesus Christ. In this day of power shortages, most of us are stupidly neglecting the greatest source of unlimited and eternally lasting power that the world has ever known. In the Baptism of Jesus, we hear the voice of the Father, by the power of his Spirit, symbolized physically in the form of a dove descending from heaven, and the Spirit is saying: "This is my beloved Son in whom I am well pleased."

Today we baptized seven infants, tiny children. But we did not baptize those children. They were baptized by the power of the Holy Spirit, as our Lord assured us. We merely acted in faith. The parents and sponsors who brought them acted in faith and in obedience to our Lord's command. Every one of them was here. By what? Through what? The power of the Holy Spirit working in the parents and sponsors who brought them! They were acting in faith, inspired by the Spirit, and through that Sacrament, that child, born into a sinful society with all of its bent toward a sinful life, completely out of contact with the God who had created it, was placed back into a Father-son relationship with God once more. That little child became a part of the fellowship of the Church of Jesus Christ and became part of our responsibility as a family of that church.

You ask: "But why baptize babies when they have no understanding of what is going on?" And I merely ask in return: "Why not?" Do you for one moment think that our understanding and knowledge is what gives the Holy Spirit power in our lives? Did these parents understand — or any of us — how those children were conceived that they brought? Did any one of us, including the parents, have any understanding about what occurred to create these new lives to live upon God's earth? Do you understand the power that brought us together as a congregation to worship this morning, along with hundreds of millions of other people throughout the world who are doing exactly the same thing? Do we understand how this faith in Christ, beginning with twelve penniless Galilean peasants, has come to countless millions from generation to generation for nearly 2,000 years? Can we understand the power that drew us here to engage in an exercise this morning that is to the Jew a stumbling block? He can't get over it. He can't get around it. He can't get through it. It's there! A tremendous stumbling block! And to the intellectuals of this world, utter idiocy.

Does these infants' lack of understanding limit the power of the Holy Spirit to come to these children through this crude vehicle of the water, and begin to exercise his power in the lives of these infants? As Paul asks: "Does Almighty God need our advice on how to conduct the business of his universe? Does he need us to tell him what he can or can't do by the power of his Holy Spirit. Do you think you're properly equipped for that task?" That is what Paul asks us.

If you want me to explain how the Holy Spirit can work in these infants, I will be very happy to oblige you, bur first I would have you engage in a little exercise. First, explain why I'm standing in this pulpit this morning, without ever in my life having wanted to. Why do I have absolute confidence that I am reaching your hearts and minds, many of you? Why am I preaching of the unlimited power of the Holy Spirit, about which I used to have a rejecting, cynical skepticism? Explain why I'm preaching this gospel without the slightest desire to do so, and that a power infinitely greater than I am is forcing me to do it. As St. Paul says: "Woe unto me, if I preach not the gospel." I'm not doing it because I want to, but because I have to. Explain all that, and then I'll be happy to explain how the Holy Spirit can work in the life of an infant.

Remember the day of Pentecost, the birthday of the church? A little group of frightened disciples was gathered together for fear of their thousands of enemies crowded into the capital city on that Festival Day, locked in that Upper Room, frightened, isolated. And then a strange power began to move through them. They sensed that they were no longer just a disorganized bunch of individuals, but that they were a fellowship, bound together by a common experience and by a passion to share that experience with everyone else in the world. As this new power laid its hold upon them, they realized that it was not their own contriving, but of God himself.

Remember how a cowardly, braggart, blowmouth, denying weakling named Peter burst out of that room and, with everything to lose — including his own life — and nothing to gain, went out and stood in the marketplace of Jerusalem and preached the gospel of Jesus Christ. Explain that, my wise friend! Explain why his Jewish enemies, as they heard him, were cut to the heart. They knew, somehow, that God's truth was being spoken, and when he finished, they asked Peter plaintively: "What can we do?" And he replied without hesitancy: "Repent and be baptized, every one of you, in the name of Jesus Christ for the forgiveness of your sins; and you shall receive the gift of the Holy Spirit." And in response, 3,000 of those who could have killed him received the Holy Spirit and were baptized, and the church was born. Explain that, my historically astute friend!

Explain this congregation of thousands that has been here for well over a century. Who did this? Leamer? Wirt? Weertz? Opperman? Valbracht? Ridiculous! There isn't a one of us who could organize a respectable ladies' sewing circle without some help. It was the Holy Spirit and his power that built this church. This congregation lived and grew in spite of us, not because of us, and it will be the Holy Spirit that, through the coming decades and centuries, if God wills, will continue to build St. John's.

Let me give you just a little vignette of the power of the Holy Spirit. Why is it, in the midst of a recession, with the specter of inflation, unemployment, a truly shaky economy facing us at every turn, that stewardship-wise, this has been the best year in our history? At the beginning of December, we needed $80,000 to meet our benevolent goals and our other expenses. It seemed a mountain of impossibility. And yet, we received *more* than $80,000. Explain this bunch of fools that laid that $80,000 on the altar of the Lord!

I was acknowledging some of the special gifts that had come in two days ago, and our Assistant Director of Music came in to me and said: "Pastor, you know, if we're going to continue to proclaim the gospel through our musicals, pageants, cantatas, and other presentations, we need a very expensive piece of equipment to add to our public address system. Our Engineer, has found one, almost new, that he can get for about half of its real cost, but I need $1,500 in order to get that. Pastor, do you know where I could dig up $1,500?" I told him frankly that I didn't know where he could dig up $1,500, but, with some misgivings, I promised to do what I could.

In almost the next letter that I had to answer, I found a check for $2,000. As some of you know, the Kings are working for a year and a half or two years in far off Saudi Arabia. The instructions on the check were that $500 should be used for their regular parish commitment, but that $1,500 should be used for "some special thing that the church needed." Knowing how Steve and Betty feel, being members of our Cathedral Choir, and knowing how they love the whole music program of our church, I picked up the phone and called Larry on the intercom and I said: "Larry, the Lord doth provide. I've got your $1,500 right on the button, so tell Carl to go out and get that mixer." O.K. Explain that to me!

You say that you've never experienced the power of the Holy Spirit, that God never speaks to you in this way? Well, beloved, I assure you that it isn't God's neglect. His Spirit is literally pounding at your heart and mind unceasingly, incessantly, and powerfully. All you have to do, as our Lord told us, is open the door.

I don't know what the mountain is that you face in your life today or how big it is. I only know that the power of the Holy Spirit — the unlimited power of the Holy Spirit — can move that mountain. And that isn't just some kind of pious hope. I say that with absolute, unequivocal, unshakable conviction.

The first year of my ministry, only a few months after ordination, I was called in an emergency to the hospital. One of the ladies in our congregation had delivered a baby, and he was not expected to live. I was asked to come and baptize the baby. I rushed to the hospital, and I look down into that incubator, after the obstetrician and pediatrician both told me there was absolutely no chance for the child's survival. I looked down at that little, twisted, blue form, and I reached my hand through a hole in the incubator and baptized the baby. I say, not I, but the Holy Spirit. And we prayed for that child's life. Despite all medical knowledge, an hour later, that baby was as healthy as any child in the nursery of that hospital. Explain that to me!

Explain how it was something other than the power of God's holy Spirit. If any one of you has another explanation, you're welcome to come up right now and tell us all about it!

The Return to Catholicity

The Seventh Sunday of Easter

TEXT: *John 17:11b — "Holy Father, keep them in thy name, which thou has given me, that they may be one, even as we are one."*

In the Name of the Father, and of the Son, and of the Holy Ghost. Amen. Beloved brothers and sisters in Christ, can you possibly understand the overwhelming sense of joy that possesses my heart and soul at this moment? I have just completed a long, long journey. It has taken me four hundred and sixty years to walk one block — from St. John's to St. Ambrose — because this Year of Our Lord One Thousand, Nine Hundred and Seventy-seven is the 460th Anniversary of the greatest revolution that have ever shaken this globe. This marks the beginning of that Reformation and that Counter-Reformation, and when I think of the hatreds, the turmoil, and the bloodshed that resulted as Christian turned upon Christian, to kill and to maim, I can only look upon this moment with holy and unrestrained rejoicing.

Little did I ever dream as I grew up as a Lutheran pastor's son in the City of Chicago that some day I would stand in the pulpit of a cathedral of the Roman tradition. May I express my heartfelt gratitude to your beloved Bishop (Maurice Dingman), the pastors of this cathedral parish, and to all of you, my friends in Christ.

Some years ago, a *New Yorker* carried a typical cartoon in which it showed a middle-aged lady lying on the psychiatrist's couch. There was a look of great agitation on her face. The doctor was saying to her: "Mrs. Murgetroyd, you just have to stop worrying about the changes that are going on in the church." Well, I hope that by this time, not only Mrs. Murgetroyd, but all of us, have stopped worrying about the changes, because we have come to realize that those changes have been instituted by Almighty God, through the power of his Holy Spirit. I also hope that we realize that the changes we have witnessed and that the changes that we will witness are evidence of the return of the church — the Church of Jesus Christ — to true catholicity.

If you should, perchance, think that I stand here as a representative of the Lutheran Church, then may I disabuse your minds by saying that there is no such thing. There is no Lutheran Church. As Martin Luther, a faithful priest of God, once said: "God forbid that any church should bear the name of such a worm as I." If I say without equivocation, not only is there no Lutheran Church, but we hold no doctrine because it is Lutheran, we celebrate no Sacrament because it is Lutheran, we participate in no liturgy because it is Lutheran, we follow no tradition because it is Lutheran. The Augsburg Confession, the first great doctrinal statement of our Lutheran tradition, addressed to the then Pontiff Leo, does not even contain the name "Luther" or the word "Lutheran." And we are not followers of Martin Luther, any more than you are followers of St. Peter or of His Holiness Pope Paul. We are disciples of Jesus Christ. We proclaim the gospel given to us through the Holy Spirit by Jesus Christ. We are part of the Church of Jesus Christ.

What tragic minunderstandings have come about through the ambiguity of our language. We talk about the churches of Christendom, when, in actuality, the word "church" should never, never be used in the plural. Certainly you realize that to speak of a group of Christians as both "Lutheran" and "catholic," or both "Roman" and "catholic" is a contradiction in terms. As St. Paul wrote to the people at Corinth: "Each one of you says, 'I belong to Paul,' or 'I belong to Apollos,' or 'I belong to Peter,' or 'I belong to Christ.'" What? Is Christ divided? Oh, yes, we can tear to shreds the visible institutional church by our prides, our sinfulness, or divisiveness and our human stupidity; but no man, nor any GROUP of men, can ever dismember the body of Christ!

Together we confess our faith by the use of the first credo of the church, written at the First Council of the Church in Nicea in the year 325. In that creed, we, in both of our traditions, state that we hold absolutely to the conviction that the church is ONE, HOLY, CATHOLIC AND APOSTOLIC. You know there is one verse in the 4th Chapter of Ephesians that contains all four of those marks of The Church: "There is one body and one Spirit, just as you are called in one hope of your calling, one Lord, one faith, one baptism, one God and Father of all, who is above all and through all and in you all."

The Oneness, for it is the same Holy Spirit of God that has called us into his Church, as our Lord said: "You have not chosen me. I have chosen you." The holiness of the church, through the redeeming, vicarious sacrifice of Jesus Christ our Lord, that makes us holy, even in the filth of our sinfulness. The catholicity — one God and Father of all, who is above all, through all, and in all, and the apostolicity in the fact that we hold the same hope of the gospel that the apostles held.

There is, however, one note of sadness in this celebration, for we have not officially joined together in communing with Christ through his Sacrament. It is the tragic irony of the history of the church that that Blessed Sacrament, with which we receive the sign and seal of our redemption, the gift that our Lord left for us to make us One Body, part of his Body, is the thing that has separated us. Traditionally, it has separated our tradition from your tradition, our tradition from the tradition of other Protestants.

In this regard, please forgive my personal impatience. I suspect that it is my background that has caused most of it. I was raised in an Irish Catholic neighborhood in the city of Chicago. One of my closest boyhood pals was one of those descendants of the Irishmen, and a faithful Roman Catholic. Despite the fact that he and I were singled out as the ringleaders in most of the juvenile delinquency that went on in that community, he was called into priesthood and I was called into the ministry.

I shall not forget the last time I saw him. It was some years ago, and it happened that we were both home during the Christmas holidays. I visited the old neighborhood, and I met him on the sidewalk. We embraced each other with laughter, glad to see each other again after all of those years. We talked about the joys of our boyhood together, and the joy that we now had, at that time, of serving the same Lord. And then, just about a year after that, I received the sad news that he had died of cancer. I was so happy that we had shared those moments together toward the end of his life here on earth.

I shall not forget the many summers I spent in the home of a devout Roman Catholic aunt, who would take me regularly to Mass and would also take me around to the various sacred shrines to which she would make a pilgrimage. People sometimes wondered why I could pray the Rosary just as easily as I could pray the "Our Father." Oh, I learned it very early in life.

And then it is the fact, also, that my daughter married a faithful Roman Catholic young man, who today is a devoted and effective Lutheran pastor in Albia, Iowa, not through my influence, not through my daughter's. He is an effective pastor, because when he entered the seminary, and all through his training, he was far ahead of the rest of the class because of the fine, Christian training that he had received in Catholic and parochial schools throughout his high school days. He is now serving the Lord because he felt, after he was married, that he had been called into the ministry.

In June, I will go to Davenport there to assist a priest in marrying my son to a beautiful, devout, Roman

Catholic girl, whom we have all learned to love. I don't know where they will worship, I only know they will worship together.

But I suppose, most of all, I remember the nearly three years that I lived, worked, trained, and ministered with a Paulist missionary priest, a fellow chaplain in the Marine Corps. I remember the Sundays in our base camp overseas when he had two Masses and I had two Services, and despite the fact that there were many men that had to be on duty and couldn't attend Services, we could have 2,000 of the 3,000 men in our regiment attending Services. We started out with a little reed organ, then with a brass quartette from our band, then with the entire regimental band.

I remember so vividly the day we landed on the black beaches of Iwo Jima, in the first hour of what was to prove to the the bloodiest battle in the history of modern warfare. I remember from the first hour to the last, some thirty days later, how we went about seeking to minister to our men, to assist with the wounded, to gather up and bury the dead. I remember how we used to crawl up through the artillery barrages, sniper fire, hails of mortar, to seek little groups of men along the line and give them Holy Communion. He heard the confessions of some of my men, and I heard the confessions of some of his, and we each bestowed the absolution of the gospel. He gave Communion to many of my men, and I gave Communion to many of his. When you are faced with matters of life and death the very next second, it does not matter who brings you Christ. It only matters that he is there, and that he's with you.

I remember the day we stood together and were decorated for valor before the whole Division — not for our valor, but for the hundreds who died, so that miraculously, impossibly, he and I came through unscathed to carry on our ministry. So we wear our medals in their honor, not ours.

Oh, yes, our theologians, you see, had a joint commission studying the Eucharist, but we have to be very patient with them. You always have to be patient with theologians.

But you'll understand why, when I went to a Catholic church in Rome, or Notre Dame in Paris, or a church in Spain, or a pretty parish church in Central America or Mexico, or the cathedral in Saigon in Vietnam, or Hong Kong, and felt no strangeness whatsoever in receiving the Sacrament with the rest of the congregation, because I know that they believe exactly what I do, that they are receiving under the rude sacrifice of Bread and Wine, the true Body and Blood of our Lord and Savior, Jesus Christ. And this is what we, in our Lutheran tradition, have maintained unshakably through these four and a half centuries, that we believe even as you do that, as Paul said: "Though we are many members, yet we are One Body in Christ."

Yes, we'll have to wait for the theologians, but you and I and your beloved Bishop, pastors, all know what Christ graciously gives us in the Sacrament. By giving us his Body, he makes us One Body, and being part of the same Body, how can we be separated? I don't care how many thousands of words Martin Luther, or Melanchthon, or St. Thomas Aquinas, or Loyola wrote about how Christ accomplishes this, the wisdom of men is still foolishness with God. You and I know that here we face the *mysterium tremendum*, that great, tremendous, sacred mystery of the Real Presence of Christ.

Last summer, the President of our particular group of Lutherans took part in your Eucharistic Congress in Philadelphia. They decided among themselves that it was not yet time for altar fellowship, so, instead, they washed one another's feet. That might be a good place to start, to wash each other's feet in humility and penitence.   .

Three years ago, I sat in an audience with the Holy Father in Rome and received his blessing with the other thousands that were gathered there. I can't help remembering the words with which he reopened the Vatican Council. He was speaking of the historic division of the Church, and he said: "If we are in any way to blame for that separation, we humbly beg God's forgiveness, and we ask pardon, too, of our brethren who feel themselves to have been injured by us." I wonder if all Lutherans could be equally gracious.

But if all of us of our Lutheran tradition are of the same spirit, along with all of you of your tradition, the time is not far off when the true oneness and the true catholicity of Christ's Church will be restored, and you and I can publicly and in good order receive his Body and Blood together. I pray earnestly for that day, and won't you join me in your prayers, also, that that day may come that Christ's prayer may be fulfilled, "That they may be one as we are one."

I greet each one of you with a holy kiss.

Now may the grace of our Lord Jesus Christ and the love of God and the communion of the Holy Ghost be with us all. Amen.

(This sermon was preached at St. Ambrose Cathedral, Des Moines, Iowa, at three Masses in observance of the 1977 Week of Prayer for Christian Unity.)